Social Media's Impact on Jamaican Mental Health

Verna D. Walker

TABLE OF CONTENTS

List of Figure..iv

List of Tables..v

Acknowledgement..vi

Dedication..vii

Abstract..viii

Chapter 1

    General Introduction..1

Chapter 2

    Research focus...9

Chapter 3

    Review of other work done..5

Chapter 4

    Research Methods..51

Chapter 5

    Findings and Interpretation of Data..61

Chapter 6

    Conclusion..83

Chapter 7

    Recommendation..90

LIST OF FIGURES

1. Overview of Social Media Use 5

2. Daily Time Spent on the Internet by Young People, 2016..21

3. Conceptual Framework Created from the Theoretical Framework 22

4. Broadened Definition of Health Conceptual Framework 24

5. Social Determinants of Mental Health Conceptual Framework 33

6. A Diagrammatic Representation of the WHO's Definition of Health............................72

7. Map of 3 counties in Jamaica..91

LIST OF TABLES

1. Characteristics of the Three Categories of Elderly, and the Ageing Transition 5

2. Human Population and Sample of Jamaica 21

3. Smith and Kington's Demand for Health Model 22

4. Leadership-Health conceptual map 24

5. Continuum of leadership behaviour 33

6. Bourne's elderly health determinant model 72

7. Map of 3 counties in Jamaica 91

ABSTRACT

Social networking (media) has radically transformed traditional communication. People can now access immediate correspondence and dialogue with others across a vast geo-political landscape. The new era of social networking brings with it benefits and disbenefits. This means that social media usage affects people's well-being. Studies have found that social networking positively influences people's mental health as well as negatively affects psychological well-being. There is no research-based consensus that social media only positively or negatively influences well-being. There are over 1.4 million social media users in Jamaica, and a search of the literature at the time of this book did not review a single study on whether social media influences Jamaicans' psychological well-being (or mental health). This lack of research-based information retards planning and the implementation of needed interventions if needs be. The objective of this book is to evaluate whether social media usage influences the mental health status of Jamaican social media users, and what is the direction of this relationship if one exists.

A web-based cross-sectional survey was used to examine the research objective. Using Survey Monkey's sample size calculator, the computed sample size was 1,068 Jamaicans. The researcher utilizes social media (WhatsApp, Facebook, X (formerly Twitter) to obtain the respondents. A team of data collectors was trained and each was responsible for collecting data from social media users for a particular parish.

Social media was found to be negatively associated with the mental health status of Jamaicans. On average, youths (ages ≤ 24 years) spent approximately 6 ± 5 hours, adults spent 4 ± 5 hours, and seniors used 3 ± 4 hours on social networking daily. This book provides research-based information on how excessive social media usage is reducing the mental health of Jamaicans. This study is the platform for understanding the effect of social media usage and should be the catalyst for needed change before the matter becomes an epidemic.

CHAPTER 1

GENERAL INTRODUCTION

Background

"Human beings are social creatures. We need the companionship of others to thrive in life, and the strength of our connections has a huge impact on our mental health and happiness" (Robinson & Smith, n.d.).

Social media is a relatively new phenomenon. Maryville University (2020) provided some historical context to the development of social media (see also, Edosomwan, et al., 2011). According to Maryville University, the first true social media platform was launched in 1997; but, that noted that the concept had its genesis on May 2, 1844. "In a sense, social media began on May 24, 1844, with a series of electronic dots and dashes tapped out by hand on a telegraph machine" (Maryville University, 2020) and this highlights the incubation of the social media and not really its true beginning. Shah (2016) clarified the historical development of social media when he articulated that social media began in 1997, but the platform was outlawed in the 1970s when computer interworking began in earnest (see also, Edosomwan, et al., 2011; Jones, 2023).

Social media has changed the landscape of communication. Before the advent of social media, communication was oral, written, and by telephone. Today, communication is instant; and it is used for many things including business, medicine, and people-to-people communication (Dhingra & Mudgal, 2019). Jones (2023) opined that "Social media is understood as the different forms of online communication used by people to create networks, communities, and collectives to share information, ideas, messages, and other content, such as videos" (p.).

The social media era has resorted to a plethora of content creators who are kings of their world, and technology is god in this space. The new era has placed a bridge between people and people, replacing people with technology in many instances. Social media content is created with little interest in the need for personal communication, and this is not in keeping with the nature of humans. Technology has for the most part replaced many of the human-to-human interactions that have resulted in a need for personal communication. This begs the question; does social media influence mental health issues including depression, loneliness and anxiety, and in general negatively influence psychological well-being?

The association between psychological well-being and social media is well-documented in the literature (Harvard T.H. Chan, School of Public Health, 2020; Ostic, et al., 2021; Zhang, et al., 2023; Valkenburg, 2022; Zsila & Reyes, 2023). Some studies have found a positive relationship between social media and psychological well-being (Cingel, et al., 2022; Harvard T.H. Chan, School of Public Health, 2020; Toma & Hancock, 2013; Vaingankar, et al., 2022; Zsila & Reyes, 2023). Others have found a reverse association between social media usage and psychological well-being (Robinson & Smith, n.d.; Zsila & Reyes, 2023). Zsila and Reyes (2023) found a two-way relationship between social media usage and psychological well-being. They argued, "It can enhance connection, increase self-esteem, and improve a sense of belonging. But it can also lead to tremendous stress, pressure to compare oneself to others, and increased sadness and isolation" (p. 201). However, the Harvard T.H. Chan, School of Public Health postulated, "Our study has brought preliminary evidence to answer this question. Using a nationally representative sample, we assessed the association of two dimensions of social media use—how much it's routinely used and how emotionally connected users are to the platforms—with three health-related outcomes: social well-being, positive mental health, and self-rated health." Robinson and Smith (n.d.), on the other hand, stated, "While many of us enjoy staying connected on social media, excessive use can fuel feelings of addiction, anxiety, depression, isolation, and FOMO. Here's how to modify your habits and improve your mood" (See also, Ostic, et al., 2021).

The literature has shown that there are two sides to the discourse of social media and mental health, which means that there is no single quantitative response to the phenomenon. Some scholars and/or writers went as far as to say that the relationship is a complex one (Nothaft, 2023; Robinson & Smith, n.d.). Those who articulated that the association is a complex one forward the two sides in the discourse. On the negative side, they believed that social media caused addiction, anxiety, loneliness, trauma, and depression (Nothaft, 2023). The positive side had increased self-esteem, bridging social capital and bonding, and suicide prevention (Ostic, et al., 2021; Nothaft, 2023). Ostic et al. (2021) provided the dual nature of social media and mental health and went further to articulate that

> The findings point to an overall positive indirect impact of social media usage on psychological well-being, mainly due to the positive effect of bonding and bridging social capital. The empirical model's explanatory power is 45.1%. This paper provides empirical evidence and robust statistical analysis that demonstrates both positive and negative effects coexist, helping to reconcile the inconsistencies found so far in the literature (p. 678766).

A model accounting for 45.1% of a phenomenon is significant and offers a real explanation of the dynamics between the two-sided relationships.

Social media occupies two sides in the mental health discourse, and it must be empirically examined in contemporary society. A study of 6595 US adolescents found a direct relationship between increased usage of social media and comorbid problems (Riehm, et al., 2019). A longitudinal study found a gender disparity between social media or television usage and its influence on mental health (Coyne, et al. (2021). Coyne et al. (2021) found that female adolescents in the United States who use more social media were at a greater risk of being suicidal than those who use it at a lower rate. However, for boys, the researchers opined, "Additionally, video game use (for boys) was associated with suicide risk when cyberbullying was also high" (p. 2324), with no information on social media and mental health phenomenon.

Why should there be a concern about the social media and mental health phenomenon? The answer to this question is embedded in the percentage of people who consume social media and the percentage of people with mental health issues in the world, particularly in the Caribbean. Statistics revealed that 61.4% of people (4.95 billion) across the globe use social media (i.e., October 2023; Datareportal, 2023). Dixon (2023), who writes for Statista, indicated that 59.4% of people across the globe use a social media platform. Although there is a disparity between the prevalence/penetration rates for social media consumption between the two authors, the difference is only 2%. See Figure 1.

Figure 1

Overview of Social Media Use

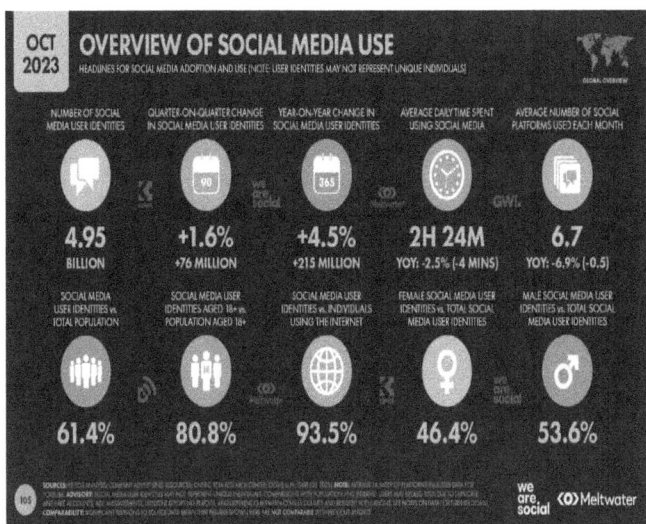

Source: Datareportal. (2023a)

The social media prevalence/penetration rate in Jamaica is significantly lower than that of the world (49.5%, which is 1.4million Jamaicans). Although the prevalence/penetration rate for social media consumption is substantially higher among those 18+ years in Jamaica, this is 18.9% lower than the global rate (Jamaica, 61.9%; globally, 80.8%). There is not only a disparity in social media prevalence/penetration rate in Jamaica and the world, but also a reversal of the gender rates. Globally, females consume less social media than males (females, 46.4%; males, 53.6%). In Jamaica, males consume more social media than males (females, 50.4%; males, 49.6%). The social media prevalence/penetration rate in the United States of America is greater than that in Jamaica (US population, 72.5%; 18+ population, 88.6%; female population) and less than globally (Datareportal, 2023c). However, the social media prevalence/penetration rate for the gender reflects a similarity between Jamaica and the United States of America (US female, 53.9%; US male, 46.1%).

Social media consumption, using prevalence/penetration rate, is highest across the globe and young people spend more on the internet than older people do. A review of the literature, as well as statistics websites that publish the prevalence/penetration rate of social media consumption, does not have disaggregation of the data by young people. However, there is one for selected nations in the world (Figure 2).

Figure 2

Daily Time Spent on the Internet by Young People, 2016

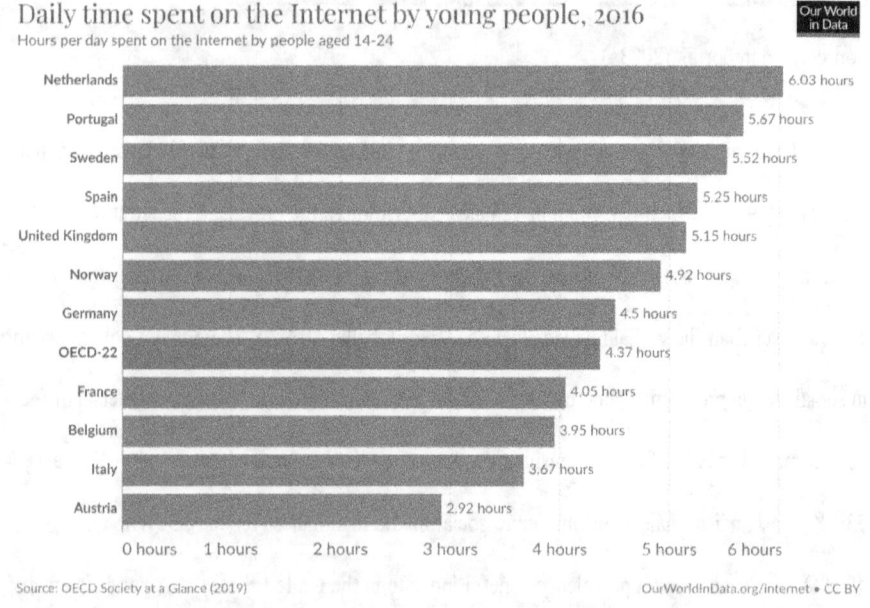

Source: Ortiz-Ospina, E. (2019).

Young people consume more social media than any other age cohort (Wong & Bottorff, 2023). The consumption of social media by young people means they are using meaningful time for meaningless things. Social media can be likened to a hard drug, it is addictive. Wong and Bottorff (2023) wrote that 39% of US young people indicated they are addicted to social media. With research finding, that social media usage influences mental health in one way, negatively or positively, it means social media usage must be brought into the public health discourse. On critically reviewing public health and social media discourses, the researcher did not find a single study at the time of writing this study on Jamaica. The current book seeks to fill the gap in the literature and provides empirical evidence on the influence of social media on the mental health of Jamaicans. This book used social media theory to quantitatively examine the relationship between social media and mental health in Jamaica.

Significance of the Study

There are many significant purposes for studying social media and mental health in Jamaica. Some of the importance that this study addresses are as follows:

1. Adds to the current literature on social media and mental health.
2. Aids in framing psychosocial policies to address the addictive nature of social media and its influence on mental health, particularly among young Jamaicans.
3. Aids in creating social intervention programs to address the social media reality in Jamaica.
4. Provides scientific evidence on the role social media plays in the mental health of Jamaicans

Purpose of the Study

One of the purposes of research is that it brings information to the forefront of people's minds. Research provides knowledge and if this is NOT promulgated to the public, the research has no value to society. This book has provided knowledge on the issue of social media usage and mental health in Jamaica; but the principal purpose of the work is to change the knowledge, attitude and practice of people. Those issues are the driving force behind the researcher using the obtained knowledge from the findings of this study to speak with the media, begin a social media awareness campaign, and framework an awareness for policymakers to include a social intervention programme for social media users.

Rationale for the Study

The rise in social media consumption can be likened to using hard drugs. Some people use social media to belittle, bully, threaten, infuriate, and incite others. Those are not healthy and cannot be encouraged to continue. Despite the value that social media have in terms of providing knowledge, and information, and educating people outside of the formal school system, there are negatives to its usage. The extent of the negative usage of social media has never been studied on the mental health of Jamaicans, and no information is 'bad information'. The rationale of this book is to provide research-based knowledge information to people and in the process begin a dialogue on behaviour modification.

Chapter two details the research focus of this book, and provides some context for the inquiry.

CHAPTER 2

RESEARCH FOCUS

Statement of the Problem

The prevalence/penetration of social media usage among Jamaicans, particularly young people, means that the addictiveness of social media must be urgently studied and findings be used to formulate effective strategies to address the issue. Social media consumption among Jamaicans is a reality and one that will not dissipate shortly because we desire it. Young Jamaicans are increasingly becoming addicted to social media and less time is spent on many other things because of the preoccupation with this communication technology. No empirical information on social media usage and mental health conditions is problematic for society, and this book needs to provide some answers to the social media paradigm.

General Research Question

The main research question of this study is, Do age, gender, and social media usage influence the mental health of Jamaicans?

Related Research Questions

The sub-research questions are as follows:

1. Is there a difference in the mental health status of social media users based on age cohorts among Jamaicans (young people, middle-aged, and elderly)?
2. Is there a difference in the mental health status of male social media users and that of female social media users?
3. Do age, gender, and social media usage influence the mental health status of Jamaicans?

Hypotheses

1. Ho (null hypothesis):

    There is no statistical difference in the mental health status of social media users based on the age cohorts of Jamaicans (young people, middle-aged, and elderly).

2. Ho (null hypothesis):

    There is no statistical difference in the mental health status of male social media users and that of female social media users.

3. Ho (null hypothesis):

    Age, gender, and social media usage are not factors in the mental health status of Jamaicans.

Definition of Terms

Age: The number of years lived by a person as of his/her last birthday.

Gender: For this book, the World Health Organization's (WHO) definition of gender is used. The WHO opined, "Gender refers to the characteristics of women, men, girls and boys that are socially constructed. This includes norms, behaviours and roles associated with being a woman, man, girl or boy, as well as relationships with each other. As a social construct, gender varies from society to society and can change over time".

Mental health: According to the World Health Organization (WHO), "Mental health is a state of mental well-being that enables people to cope with the stresses of life, realize their abilities, learn well and work well, and contribute to their community. It is an integral component of health and well-being that underpins our individual and collective abilities to make decisions, build relationships and shape the world we live in" (WHO, 2022a). This book uses the conceptualization of the WHO on mental health.

Social Media: Jones's (2023) definition of social media is used in this book. Jones opined, "Social media is understood as the different forms of online communication used by people to create networks, communities, and collectives to share information, ideas, messages, and other content, such as videos."

Psychological well-being: Psychological well-being is the core feature of mental health (Tang, et al., 2019). Dhanabhakyam & Sarath (2023) postulated, "Psychological well-being is a multifaceted and multidimensional construct that encompasses an individual's overall happiness, satisfaction with life, and mental and emotional health" (p. 603). Psychological well-being is widely used and validated in the literature to measure mental health and is equally extended to assess well-being (Abbott, et al., 206; Burns, 2016; Ryff & Keyes, 1995; Ryff & Singer, 2006; Ryff, 1989a, 1989b, 1989c; Seifert, 2005; Springer & Hauser, 2006; Springer, et al., 2006).

Limitations of the Study

Several limitations emerged in this book. They are as follows:

1. Non-generalizability: The study is not generalized to all Jamaicans because data were. collected from social media users who were 18 years and older. The exclusion of those below 18 years from this book does not provide research-based information on substantive a sub-population in Jamaica.

2. Instrumentation: The use of the 18-item Ryff's Psychological Well-being Scale (PWBS) was not able to assess the multidimensionality of the mental health of Jamaicans, particularly because the six categories of the general index was not suitable and appropriate to measure the sub-scales. The researcher chose to use the 18-item Ryff's PWBS because Jamaicans do not like to read lengthy materials, which would increase the non-response rate.

3. Population characteristics: There are no published statistics from any reputable statistical agency in Jamaica on the population characteristics of social media users across the parishes. This retards the accuracy and ability of the researcher to scientifically determine social media users.

Chapter three which comes next explores the extensive review done on other work to include analyses of extant literature related to the book title.

CHAPTER 3

REVIEW OF OTHER WORK DONE

This chapter examines the literature surrounding the topic, Do Age, Gender, and Social Media Usage Influence the Mental Health Status of Jamaicans? The chapter presents the conceptual and theoretical framework that outlines the body of work in the areas of social media usage, health status and well-being, age, gender, and mental health status. Although the topic is Jamaicans, this chapter presents a worldview on the issues including the Jamaican perspectives. The historical and contemporary perspectives on social media usage and health were used to establish the gap in the literature. The gap in the literature was that there is no evidence on whether social media usage influences the mental health status of Jamaicans, and what the direct of the association if any existed.

The researcher employed an objectivistic epistemology research design for this book, which explained the focus on a research-based evidence framework. The objectivistic epistemological underpinning of this book justifies the use of a theoretical and conceptual framework. In this chapter, the discussion begins with a theoretical and conceptual framework followed by the main concepts of the study. The main concepts were health and well-being, psychological well-being, mental health, age, and gender.

The theoretical framework is the human capital theory, and how Michael Grossman (1972) used this to objectively measure factors that influence good health status. Those factors later became known as social determinants of health. It is the Commission on Social Determinants that first coined the term social determinants of health as what was previously known as factors or correlates of health. This theoretical underpinning explains the conceptual framework that was used to structure their study. A conceptual map is presented in this book as it provides the overall structure of the study.

Conceptual and Theoretical Framework

A theoretical framework outlines the assumptions and relationships that are explored in a study (Crotty, 2005; Merriam & Tisdell, 2016). The conceptual framework, on the other hand, provides the overall structure of the study (Ravtich & Riggan, 2017). According to Crotty (2005), "[The] Theoretical perspective: the philosophical stance informing the methodology and thus providing a context for the process and grounding its logic and criteria (p. 3). The idea is clear that the theoretical framework is subsumed in the conceptual framework. This book provides a theoretical framework that aided the creation of a conceptual framework, and this is summarized in a conceptual map.

The Human Capital Model (HCM) of demand for health is the theoretical framework employed in this book. HCM views durable capital stock that can yield an output of healthy time (Bleakley 2010; Grossman, 1972, 1999). The HCM is a product like any other that can be improved or otherwise based on the behaviour of the people. One of the principles of HCM is that "Individuals inherit an initial amount of this stock that depreciates with age and can be increased by investment" (Grossman, 1979, p. 102). Grossman was of the view that in general people begin with good health, and with age, this decreases; and that people's investment can increase as well as reduce the initial good health status.

The Human Capital Model of the demand for health was used by Grossman (1972) to develop a mathematical expression for good health status. He was able to establish a theoretical framework for the biological, psychological, and sociological conditions that influence good health outcomes for people. Grossman theorized that current health status (good health status), Ht, is determined by past health status, Ht-1, and other factors.

These are expressed in Equation [1] or Figure 2:

$$Ht = f(Ht\text{-}1, Go, Bt, MCt, ED) \quad \text{...} \quad (1)$$

Equation 1 depicts the five factors influencing the health outcomes of people. The predicted factors were Go, Bt, ED, and MCt, with Ht-1 being the initial health that people were born with. Ht was the dependent variable that was influenced by the predictors, which were previously stated.

Where:

Ht – current health in period t,

the stock of health (Ht-1) in a period before time t,

But – smoking and excessive drinking, and good personal health behaviours (including exercise – Go),

MCt, – use of medical care,

education of each family member (ED), and

all sources of household income (including current income).

Grossman's pioneer work was the first study to quantitatively assess health and brought health from a concept to an operational phenomenon. Smith and Kington (1997a) expanded on the early work of Grossman (1972). They brought in additional factors of good health status, see Equation 2 or Figure 3).

$$Ht = H^*(Ht\text{-}1, Pmc, Po, ED, Et, Rt, At, Go) \quad \text{................................} \quad (2)$$

Where Ht is the current health status (good health status),

Ht-1 is the initial health status at birth,

Pmc is the price of medical care,

Po is the price of other inputs,

ED is the education of each,

It is a family member of all sources of household income,

Go is family background or genetic endowments,

Rt is retirement-related income, and

At is asset income.

Smith and Kington were not finished with explaining factors that influence the good health status of people. So, they expanded on their earlier work (1997b). The platform was set to evaluate the good health status of people. The term factor was used to explain Gr'ssman's Smith and K'ngton's works. The term social determinants of health was first used by the Commission on Social Determinants of Health (CSDH) and this was spearheaded by Solar and Irwin (2004, 2005; see also, Commission on Social Determinants of Health, 2008). Scholars have used the term social determinants of health to explain factors that influence/determine health outcomes (Braveman, & Gottlieb, 2014; Graham, 2004; Irwin & Scali, 2007). Before the CSDH, the terminology was factors (Grossman, 1997, 1999; Smith & Kington, 1997a, 1997b) and correlates (Hambleton, et al., 2005).

Outside of the conceptual choices used by scholars, many have conducted studies on the social determinants of health (Bourne 2008a, 2008b, 2009a, 2009b, 2009c, 2009d, 2009e, 2009f; 2010a, 2010b, 2010c, 2013a, 2013b; Bourne & McGrowder, 2009a, 2009b, 2010; Bourne & Rhule, 2009; Graham, 2004; Kelly et al., 2007). The theoretical framework from the works of

Grossman (1972), Smith and Kington (1997a, 1997b), and others can be conceptually framed in Figure 3, below:

Conceptual Map

The conceptual map (Figure 3) presents the overall structure of this study.

Figure 3

Conceptual Framework Created from the Theoretical Framework

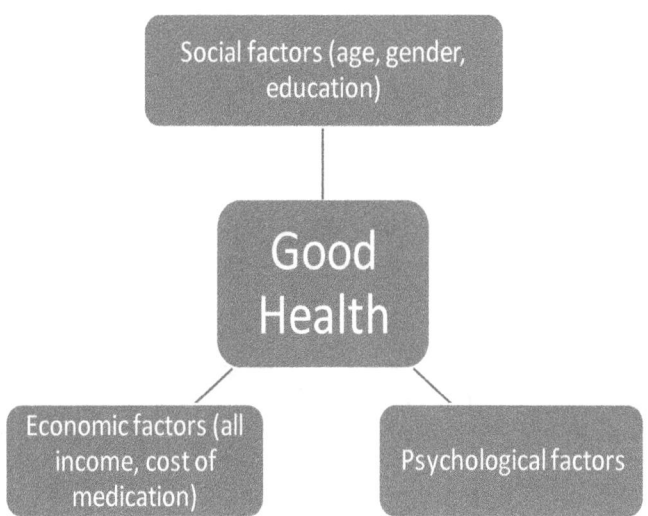

In the literature, health is subjectively measured by way of self-reported happiness, self-reported health, self-reported quality of life, and objectively by way of life expectancy (or mortality pattern). The issue of subjective health or well-being is discussed further in this chapter of the book. However, the definition of health comprises biological (physical health), social, and psychological well-being, so, the conceptual framework created from the theoretical framework can be disaggregated to be (see Figure 4).

Figure 4

Broadened Definition of Health Conceptual Framework

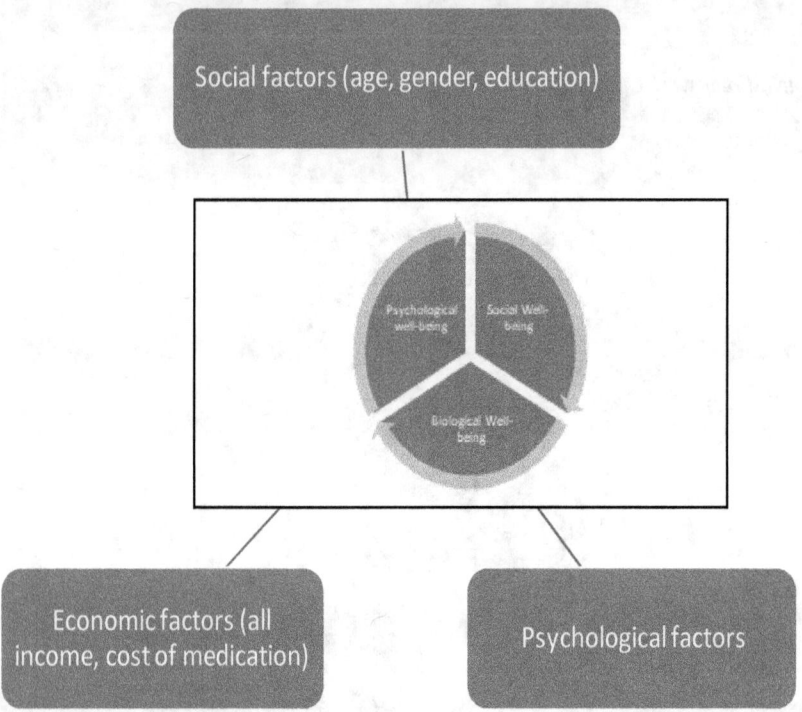

Based on the extended view of good health status, this book extracts psychological well-being (which is mental health) to create a conceptual framework. The literature established that social media influences mental health and that age and gender are social determinants of health; then this book the researcher creates a single conceptual framework with two separate frameworks. For this book, the researcher's conceptual framework is age, gender, and social media usage influence psychological well-being or mental health (see Figure 5).

Figure 5

Social Determinants of Mental Health Conceptual Framework

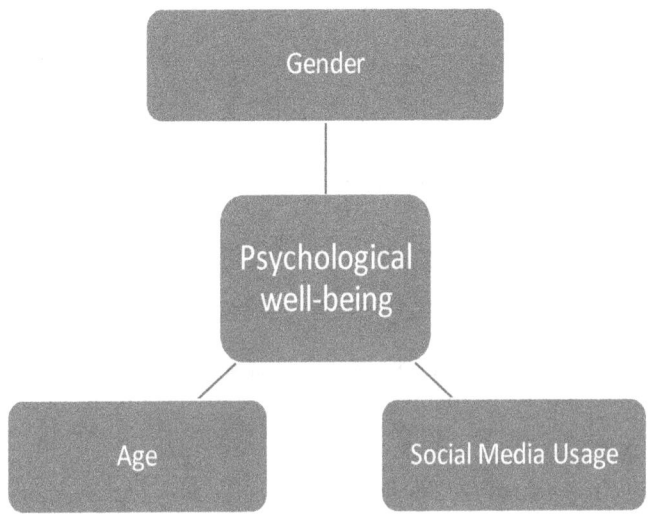

Figure 5 can be depicted as a mathematical equation as outlined by Grossman (1972) or Smith and Kington (1997a, 1997b) as follows:

$$PWB = f(A, G, SMU) \quad \text{............................Equation [3]}$$

Where

PWB denotes psychological well-being (or mental health)

A symbolizes the age of respondents at the time t

G is the gender of the respondents

SMU is social media usage by Jamaicans.

This book quantitatively tests whether age, gender, and social media usage are social determinants (factors or correlates) of the psychological well-being of Jamaicans. The remainder of this chapter (Chapter 2) examines the three main concepts of the conceptual framework (subjective well-being including psychological well-being, gender, social media usage, and age of Jamaicans).

Health and Well-being

The concept of health according to the WHO is multifaceted. "Health is a state of complete physical, mental and social well, and not merely being the absence of disease or infirmity" (Whang 2006, 153; WHO, 1948a, 1948b). From the WHO's perspective, health status is an indicator of well-being (See also, Crisp, 2005). Well-being for some, therefore, is a state of happiness – positive feeling status and life satisfaction (see for example, Diener, 1984; Diener et al., 1985; Easterlin 2003) satisfaction of preferences or desires, health or prosperity of an individual (Crips, 2005; Jones, 2001; Diener & Suh, 1997; Whang, 2006), or what psychologists refer to as positive effects (Headey & Wooden, 2004). Simply put, well-being is subjectively what is 'good' for each person (see, for example, Crisp, 2005). It is sometimes connected with good health. Crisp explained this when he said, "When discussing the notion of what makes life good for the individual living that life, it is preferable to use the term 'well-being' instead of 'happiness" (Crisp, 2005), which explains the rationale for this project utilizing the term *well-being* and not *good health*.

To forward an understanding of what constitutes well-being or ill-being, a system must be instituted that will allow us to coalesce a measure that will unearth peoples' sense of overall quality of life from either economic-welfarism (see Becker et al., 2004) or psychological theories (Diener, 2000; Diener et al., 1997; Headey & Wooden, 2004; Kashdan, 2004). This must be done with the general construct of a complex man. Economists like Smith and Kington (1997a, 1997b), Stutzer and Frey (2003) as well as Engel (1960, 1977, 1978, 1980) believed that the state of man's well-being is not only influenced by his/her biological state but is always dependent on his/her environment, economic and sociologic conditions. Some studies and academics have sought to analyze this phenomenon subjectively by way of general personal happiness, self-rated well-being, positive moods and emotions, agony, hopelessness, depression, and other psychosocial indicators (Arthaud-day et al. 2005; Diener, 1984; Diener et al., 1999; Skevington et al., 1997).

An economist, Easterlin, studying happiness and income, of all social scientists, found an association between the two phenomena (Easterlin 2001a, 2001b, 2003, 2004), (see also Stutzer & Frey, 2003). He began with a statement that "the relationship between happiness and income is puzzling" (Easterlin 2001a, p. 465), and found people with higher incomes were happier than those with lower incomes – he referred to as a correlation between subjective well-being and income (see also, Stutzer & Frey 2003, p. 8). He did not cease at this juncture but sought to justify this reality, when he said that "those with higher income will be better able to fulfil their aspirations and, other things being equal, on an average, feel better off" (Easterlin, 2001a, p. 472). Well-being, therefore, can be explained outside of welfare theory and/or purely on objectification- objective utility (See for example, Kimball & Willis, 2005; Stutzer & Frey, 2003).

Whereas Easterlin found a bivariate relationship between subjective well-being and income, Stutzer and Frey revealed that the association is a non-linear one. They concretized the position by explaining that "In the data set for Germany, for example, the simple correlation is 0.11 based on 12, 979 observations" (Stutzer and Frey 2003, 9). Nevertheless, from Stutzer and

Frey's findings, a position association does exist between subjective well-being and income despite differences over linearity or non-linearity.

The issue of well-being is embodied in three theories – (1) Hedonism, (2) Desire, and (3) Objective List. Using 'evaluative hedonism', well-being constitutes the greatest balance of pleasure over pain (see for example, Crisp 2005; Whang 2006, p. 154). With this theorizing, well-being is just personal pleasantness, which represents that the more pleasantries an individual receives, he/she will be better off. The very construct of this methodology is the primary reason for criticism of its approach (i.e. 'experience machine'), which gave rise to other theories. Crisp (2005) using the work of Thomas Carlyle described the hedonistic structure of utilitarianism as the 'philosophy of swine' because this concept assumes that all pleasure is on par. He summarized this adequately by saying that "… whether they [are] the lowest animal pleasures of sex or the highest of aesthetic appreciation" (Crisp 2005, p.).

The desired approach, on the other hand, is on a continuum of experienced desires. This is popularized by welfare economics. Economists see well-being as constituting satisfaction of preference or desires (Crisp, 2005, p. 7; Whang, 2006, p. 154), which makes for the ranking of preferences and their assessment by way of money. People are made better off if their current desires are fulfilled. Despite this theory's strengths, it has a fundamental shortcoming, the issue of addiction. This is forwarded by the possible addictive nature of consuming 'hard drugs' because of the summative pleasure it gives to the recipient.

Objective list theory: This approach in measuring well-being lists items not merely because of pleasurable experiences nor on 'desire-satisfaction' but that every good thing should be included such as knowledge and friendship. It is a concept influenced by Aristotle, and "developed by Thomas Hurka (1993) as perfectionism" (Crisp, 2005). According to this approach, the constituent of well-being is an environment of perfecting human nature. What goes on an 'objective list' is based on the reflective judgement or intuition of a person. A criticism of this technique is elitism (Crisp, 2005); since this approach assumes that certain things are good for people. Crisp (2005) provided an excellent rationale for this limitation when he said that "...even if those people will not enjoy them, and do not even want them" (p.).

In Arthaud-day et al work, applying structural modelling, subjective well was found to constitute "(1) cognitive evaluations of one's life (i.e., life satisfaction or happiness); (2) positive affect; and (3) negative affect." Subjective well-being, therefore, is the individual's viewpoint. If an individual feels his/her life is going well, then we need to accept this as the person's reality. One of the drawbacks to this measurement is that it is not summative, and lacks generalizability.

Studies have shown that subjective well-being can be measured on a community level (Bobbit et al.2005; Lau 2005; Boelhouwer and Stoop 1999) or a household level (Lau 2005; Diener 1984), whereas other experts have sought to use empiricism (biomedical indicators - absence of disease symptoms, life expectancy; and an economic component - Gross Domestic Product per capita; welfarism - utility function).

Powell's (1997) paper titled *'Measures of Quality of life and subjective well-being'* argued that psychological well-being is a component of quality of life. He believed that this measurement in particular for the older, must include the Life Satisfaction Index, as this approach constitutes several items based on "cognitively based attitudes toward life in general and more emotion-based judgment"(Powell 1997). Powell addressed this from two dimensions. Where those means are relatively constant over time while seeking to unearth changes in the short-run, 'for example an intervention', procedures that mirror changed states may be preferable. This can be assessed by way of a twenty-item Positive and Negative Affect Schedule or from a ten-item Philadelphia Geriatric Centre Positive Affect and Negative Affect Scale (Powell 1997).

In a reading titled '*Objective measures of well-being and the cooperation production problem*', Gaspart (1998) provided arguments that support the rationale behind the objectification of well-being. His premise for objective quality of life is embedded within the difficulty as it relates to consistency of measurement when subjectivity is the construct of operationalization. This approach takes precedence because an objective measurement of concept is of exactness as non-objectification; therefore, the former receives priority over any subjective preferences. He claimed that for well-being to be comparable across individuals, populations and communities, there is a need for empiricism.

Gaspart (1998) discussed several economic theories (Equal Income Walrasian equilibria, objective egalitarianism, Pareto efficiency; Wefarism), which saw the paper expounding on several mathematical theorems to quantify the quality of life. Such a stance proposes that humans are predictable, rational from which we can objectify their plans. The very axioms cited by Gaspart emphasized a particular set of assumptions that he used to finalise a measurement of well-being for man who is a complex social animal. The researcher points to a sentence that was written by Gaspart that speaks to the difficulty of objective quality of life; he wrote, "So its objectivism is already contaminated by post-welfare, opening the door to a mixed approach, in which preferences matter as well as objective well-being" (Gaspart, 1998, p.). Another group of scholars emphasized the importance of measuring well-being outside welfarism and/or purely objectification when they said "Although GDP per capita is usually used as a proxy for the quality of life in different countries, material gain is only one of many aspects of life that enhance economic well-being" (Becker et al., 2004, p. 1), and that well-being depends on both the quality and the quantity of life lived by the individual (see also Easterlin, 2001; Bourne,

2009f). This is affirmed in a study carried out by Lima and Nova (2006), which found happiness, general life satisfaction, social acceptance and actualizations are all directly related to GDP per capita for a geographic location (see Lima & Nova 2006, 9). Even though in Europe these were found not to be causal, income provides some predictability of subjective well-being more so in poor countries than in wealthy nations. (see Lima & Nova, 2006, p. 11)

It is understood that GDP per capita speaks of the market economic resources which are produced domestically within a particular geographic space (Bourne, 2009f). So increased production in goods and/or services may generate excess which can then be exported, and vital products (such as vaccination, sanitary products, vitamins, iron and other commodities) can be purchased that can improve the standard of living and quality of the life of the same people over the previous period. One scholar (Caldwell 1999) has shown that life expectancies are usually higher in countries with high GDP per capita, which means that income can purchase better quality products, which indirectly affects the length of years lived by people. This reality could explain why in an economic recession, war and violence when the economic growth is lower (or even non-existent) there is a lower life expectancy. Some of the reasons for these justifications are the government's unavailability to provide for an extensive population in the form of nutritional care, public health and health-care services. Good health is, therefore, linked to economic growth, which further justifies why economists use GDP per capita as an objective valuation of the standard of living (Bourne, 2009f); and why income should indefinitely be a component in the analysis of health status. There is another twist to this discourse a country's GDP per capita may be low, but the life expectancy is high because health care is free for the population. Despite this fact, material living standards undoubtedly affect the health status and well-being of a people, as well as the level of females' educational attainment.

Ringen (1995) in a paper titled '*Well-being, measurement, and Preferences*' argued that non-welfarist approaches to measuring well-being are possible despite its subjectivity. The direct approach for well-being computation through the utility function according to Ringen is not a better quantification, as against the indirect method (i.e., using social indicators). The stance taken was purely from the vantage point that *utility* is a function 'not of goods and preferences' but of products and 'taste'. The constitution of well-being is based on choices. Choices are a function of individual assets and options. With this premise, Ringen forwarded arguments which show that people's choices are sometimes 'irrational', which makes for the departure from empiricism.

Well-being can be computed from either the direct (i.e. consumption expenditure) or the indirect (i.e. disposable income) approach (Ringen 1995, 8). The former is calculated using consumption expenditure, whereas the latter uses disposable income. Ringen noted that to use income as a proxy for well-being, we must assume that (1) income is the only resource, and (2) all persons operate in identical marketplaces. On the other hand, the direct approach has two key assumptions. These are (1) what we can buy is what we can consume and (2) and that what we can consume, is an expression of well-being. From Ringen's monograph, the assumptions are limitations.

In presenting potent arguments in favour of non-empiricism in the computation of well-being, Ringen highlighted several drawbacks to welfarism. According to Ringen,

> Utility is not a particularly good criterion for well-being since it is a function not only of circumstances and preferences but also of expectations. In the measurement of well-being, respect for personal preferences is best sought in non-welfarist approaches that

have the quality of preference neutrality; ... As soon, as preferences are brought into the concept of well-being cannot but be subjective (Ringen, 1995, p. 11)

The difficulties in using empiricism to quantify well-being have not only been forwarded by Ringen, as O'Donnell and Tait (2003) were equally forthwith in arguing there were challenges in measuring quality of life quantitatively. O'Donnell and Tait believed that health is a primary indicator of well-being. Hence, self-rated health status is a highly reliable proxy of health which "successfully crosses cultural lines" (O'Donnell & Tait, 2003, p. 20). They argued *that self-reported health status* can be used as they found that all the respondents with chronic diseases indicated that their health was very poor.

To capture the state of the quality of life of humans, we are continuously and increasingly seeking to ascertain more advanced methods that will allow us to encapsulate a quantification of well-being that is multidimensional and multifaceted (Pacione, 2003). Therefore, an operational definition of well-being that sees the phenomenon on a single dimension such as physical health (Simons, & Baldwin, 2021), medical perspective (Farquhar 1995; Simons, & Baldwin, 2021).), material (Lipsey, 1999) and excluded indicators such as crime, education, leisure facilities, housing, social exclusion and the environment (Campbell, et al., 1976; Pacione, 2003), as well as subjective indicators, cannot be an acceptable holistic measurement of this construct. This suggests that well-being is simply not a single space; and so, the traditional biomedical conceptual definitions of well-being exclude many individual satisfaction and in the process reduce the tenets of a superior coverage of quality of life.

One writer noted that the environment positively influences the quality of life (Pacione 2003, 20) of people; to establish validity and reliability of well-being, empirical data must include issues relating to the environment. The quality of the environment is a utilized condition in explaining elements of the quality of life of people. Air and water quality through industrial fumes, toxic waste, gases and other pollutants affect environmental quality. This is directly related to the maintenance or lack thereof of societal and personal well-being (Pacione, 2003).

Studies have conclusively shown that environmental issues such as industrial fumes and gases, poor solid waste management, mosquito infestation and poor housing are likely to result in physiological conditions like respiratory tract infections (for example lung infection), and asthma.

According to Langlois and Anderson (2002), approximately 30 years ago, seminal studies conducted by Smith (1973, 2) "proposed that well-being be used to refer to conditions that apply to a population generally, while the quality of life should be limited to individuals' subjective assessments of their lives ..." They argue that a distinction between the two variables has been lost with time. From Langlois and Anderson's monograph, during the 1960s and 1970s, well-being was approached from a quantitative assessment by the use of GDP or GNP (also See, Becker, Philipson and Soares 2004), and unemployment rates; this they refer to as a "rigid approach to the [enquiry of the subject matter] subject". According to Langlois and Anderson (2002), the positivist approach to the methodology of well-being was objectification, an assessment that was highly favoured by Andrews and Withley (1976) and Campbell et al., 1976.

In measuring the quality of life, some writers have thought it fitting to use Gross Domestic Product per capita (i.e., GDP per capita) which they referred to as the standard of living (Hanson, 1986; Lipsey, 1999; Summers & Heston, 1995). According to Summers and Heston (1995), "The index most commonly used until now to compare countries' material well-being is their GDP_{POP}." The United Nations Development Programme has expanded on the material well-being definition forwarded primarily by economists and has included life expectancy and educational attainment (Human Development Reports, 2005, p. 341) and other social indicators (Diener, 1984; Diener & Suh, 1997). This operational definition of well-being has become increasingly popular in the last twenty-five years but given the expanded definition of health as cited by the WHO (1948a, 1948b), well-being must be measured in a more comprehensive manner than using material well-being as seen by economists.

Even though quality of life extends beyond the number of years of schooling and material well-being, generally well-being is substantially construed as an economic phenomenon. Embedded within this construct of a measure is the emphasis on economic resources, and we have already established that man's well-being is multifaceted. Hence, any definition of the quality of life of people cannot just simply analyze spending or the creation of goods and/or services that are economically exchangeable, several years of schooling and life expectancy but this must include the psychosocial conditions of the people within their natural environment.

GDP is the coalesced sum of all economic resources of people in a certain topography, so this does not capture the psychosocial state of the man in attaining the valued GDP. By this approach, we may arrive at a value that is higher than in previous periods, making it seem as though people are doing very well. However, with this increase in GDP, this single component is insufficient to determine well-being. The increase in GDP may be by (1) more working hours, (2) higher rates of pollution and environmental conditions, (3) psychological fatigue, (4) social exclusion, (5) human 'burnout', (6) reduction in freedom, (7) unhappiness, (8) chronic and acute diseases and so forth. Summers and Heston (1995) note that "However, GDP_{POP} is an inadequate measure of countries' immediate material well-being, even apart from the general practical and conceptual problems of measuring countries' national outputs." Generally, from that perspective, the measurement of quality of life is, therefore, highly economic and excludes the psychosocial factors, and if quality of life extends beyond monetary objectification.

In developing countries, Camfield (2003) in looking at well-being from a subjective vantage point notes that Diener (1984) argues that subjective well-being constitutes the existence of positive emotions and the absence of negative ones within a space of general satisfaction with life. According to Camfield, Cummins' (1997) perspective subsumed 'subjective and objective measures of material well-being' along with the absence of illnesses, efficiency, social closeness, security, place in the community, and emotional well-being, which implies that "life's satisfaction" comprehensively envelopes subjective well-being.

Diener (2000) in an article titled 'Subjective Well-being: The Science of Happiness and a Proposal for a National Index' theorizes that the objectification of well-being is embodied within satisfaction of life. He points to a construct of well-being called happiness. He cited that:

> People's moods and emotions reflect online reactions to events happening to them. Each individual also makes broader judgments about his or her life as a whole, as well as about domains such as marriage and work. Thus, there are several separable components of SWB [subjective well-being]: life satisfaction (global judgments of one's life), satisfaction with important domains (e.g., work satisfaction), positive affect (experiencing many pleasant emotions and moods), and low levels of negative affect (experiencing few unpleasant emotions and moods). In the early research on SWB, researchers studying the facets of happiness usually relied on only a single self-report item to measure each construct (Diener, 2000, p. 34).

Diener's theorizing on well-being encapsulates more than the marginalized stance of other academics and researchers who enlightened the discourse with economic, psychosocial, or subjective indicators. He shows that quality of life is multifaceted and coalescing economic, social, psychological and subjective indicators is far more reaching in ultimately measuring well-being. This work shows a construct that can be used to operationalize a more multidimensional variable, well-being, which widens the tenet of the previous operational definition on the subject. From the theorizing of various writers, well-being is multidimensional, multidisciplinary and multispatial. Some writers emphasize the environmental components of the subject matter (Pacione, 1984; Smith, 1973), psychosocial aspects (Clarke et al., 2000) and from a social capital vantage point (Glaeser, 2001; Putnam, 1995; Woolcock, 2001).

According to Smith and Kington (1997a), using $H_t = f(H_{t-1}, P_m, G_o, B_t, MC_t, ED, \bar{A}_t,)$ to conceptualize a theoretical framework for "stock of health" noted that health in period t, Ht, is the result of health preceding this period (H_{t-1}), medical care (MC_t), good personal health (G_o), the price of medical care (P_m), and bad ones (B_t), and a vector of family education (ED), and all sources of household income ($\bar{A}_t$). Embedded in this function is the well-being that an individual enjoys (or does not enjoy) (see Smith & Kington, 1997a, pp. 159-160).

In seeking to operationalize well-being, the United Nations Development Programme (UNDP) in the Human Development Reports (1997, 2000) conceptualized human development as a "process of widening people's choice as well as the level of achieving well-being". Embedded within this definition is the emphasis on materialism in interpreting the quality of life. According to the UNDP's Human Development (1993), the human development index (HDI) "...is a normative measure of a desirable standard of living or a measure of the level of living", which speaks to the subjectivity of this valuation irrespective of the inclusion of welfarism (i.e. gross domestic product (GDP) per capita). The HDI constitutes adjusted educational achievement (E= a_1* literacy + a_2 * years of schooling, where a1, = 2/3 and a2 = 1/3), life expectancy (demographic modelling) and income (W $(9y) = 1/(1 - e) * y^{1-e}$). The function W(y) denotes "utility or well-being derived from income". This income component of the HDI is a national average (i.e. GDP per capita, which is adjusted for income distribution ($W^*(y) = W(y)\{1 - G\}$), where G = Gini coefficient). In wanting to disaggregate the HDI within a country, the UNDP (1993) noted that data are not available for many countries, which limits the possibility.

An economist writing on 'objective well-being' summarized the matter simply by stating that "…one can adopt a mixed approach, in which the satisfaction of subjective preferences is taken as valuable too" (Gaspart, 1998, p. 111) (see also Cummins, 1997a, 2001), which is the premise upon which this paper was compliant in keeping with this multidimensional construct, well-being. Well-being, therefore, for this paper is the overall health status of people, which includes access to and control over material resources, environmental and psychosocial conditions, and per capita consumption. The definition of health, which is widely referred to as well-being, comes from the Preamble to the Constitution of the WHO (1948a, 1948b) and is a multidimensional construct. For this book, the researcher uses a diagram that aptly captures the WHO's definition of health (Figure 6):

Figure 6

A Diagrammatic Representation of the WHO's Definition of Health

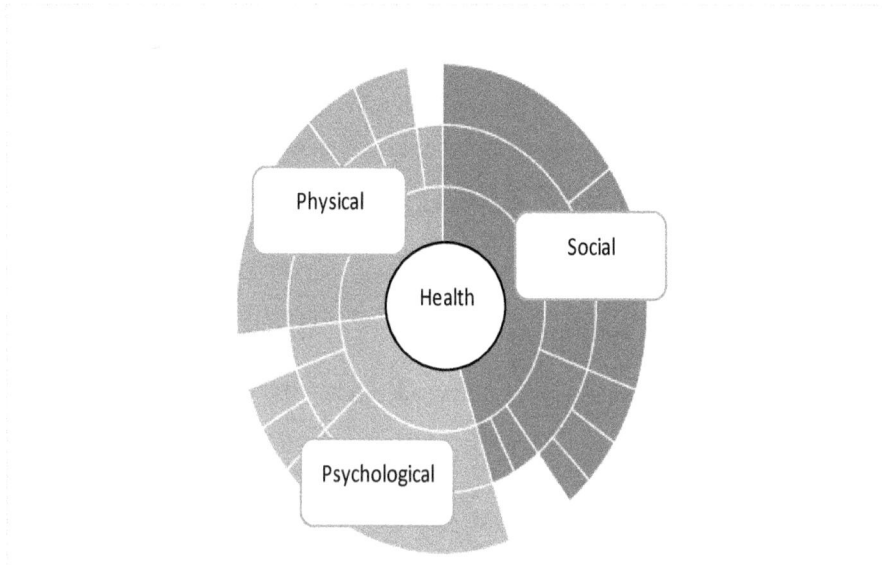

Psychological Well-being and Health

Psychological well-being is a positive mental status and functioning well, which includes happiness and life satisfaction (Diener, 1985, 2000; Diener, et al., 2009; Ruggeri, et al., 2020). Diener et al. (2009) referred to it as positive and negative feelings as well as positive thinking. There is consensus around the general concept of psychological well-being, which is mental health status, such as happiness, positive feelings, and life satisfaction. Psychological well-being is one of the dimensions of health (WHO, 1948a, 1948b), and Tan et al. (2019) indicated that it is a 'core feature' of mental health. The World Health Organization (WHO) conceptualizes mental health as a "state of well-being in which the individual realizes his or her abilities, can cope with the normal stresses of life, can work productively and fruitfully, and …[can] to contribute to his or her community." This means that psychological well-being scales are suitable and appropriate for assessing mental health status.

Psychological well-being is positive health or good mental health (Ryff, et al., 2004). This conceptualization holds the key to understanding the two types of psychological well-being (Hedonic and Eudaimonic). Hedonic well-being deals with the subjective feelings of happiness. Carruthers & Hood (2004) note that hedonic well-being has two components, an affective and a cognitive component. The affective component deals with positive and negative feelings and the cognitive component looks at satisfaction with life. Eudaimonic well-being refers to the purpose of psychological well-being. Carol Ryff developed and spent years assessing the psychological well-being of different populations (1989a, 1989b, 2014; Ryff & Keyes, 1995).

The psychological well-being scale developed by Ryff measures the concept of happiness, life satisfaction, and positive affect (Ryff, 1989a, 2014). The original indexation had internal consistencies of 0.86 to 0.93 (Ryff, 1989a). The scale at the time comprised six scales. Ryff's psychological well-being scale has a different number of items. One comprises 18 items (short form) and another 42-84 items (long form). Ryff's Psychological well-being scale has been validated in different nations including China (Cheng & Chan, 2005; Gao & McLellan, 2018; Li, 2014; Kline, 2015), Sweden (Garcia, et al., 2023; Lindfors, et al., 2006), Canada (Clarke, et al., 2001), Iran (Khanjaniet al., 2014), Portugal (Fernandes et al., 2010), and Italy (Sirigatti et al., 2009).

Although Ryff's psychological well-being scale has been validated in various nations, there are criticisms levied against it, particularly the 18-item version. A group of researchers indicated that the discriminant validity of the 18-item scale is questionable as five of the six items had high cross-loadings (Hsu, et al., 2017). Hambleton and Jones (1993) noted that the true score upon which the Classical Test Theory (CTT) is based showed signs that they do not reflect the responses of the participants. Such a fact decreases the predictability of the specific items. However, Garcia, et al.'s (2023) and Lindfors, et al.'s (2006) works validate the suitability and appropriateness of the 18-item scale.

Bradburn (1969) developed a different measure to assess psychological well-being, which is referred to as the Affect Balance Scale. Bradburn's scale comprises two components. These are one, Positive affective, and two,. Negative affect, with each having 5 items. The responses were either yes or no. Bradburn's scale measured happiness. Like Ryff's psychological well-being scale, there were criticisms against Bradburn's scale (McDowell & Praught, 1982). One of the criticisms of Bradburn's psychological scale was it did not adequately summarize the data (Perkinson, et al., 1994). This statistical weakness explains the development of scales. Despite this criticism, Macintosh (1998) argued that is it widely validated and utilized to assess social psychological well-being in many nations (see also, George, 1981; Glatzer & Gulyas, 2014; Harding, 1982; Helmes, et al., 2010; Sauer & Warland, 1982). The many scholars who examined psychological well-being concur that it assesses the mental health status of a human.

Mental Health Status across the Globe

In 2019, the World Health Organization reported that 12.5% of people across the globe live with a mental disorder (WHO, 2022b). The WHO was referring to anxiety disorder, depression, post-traumatic stress disorder (PTSD), bipolar disorder, schizophrenia, disruptive behaviour and dissocial disorders, eating disorders, disruptive behaviour and dissocial disorders, and neurodevelopmental disorders. The WHO continued, "In 2020, the number of people living with anxiety and depressive disorders rose significantly because of the COVID-19 pandemic."

The National Center for Chronic Disease Prevention and Health Promotion, Division of Population Health (2023) reported that 20% of US adults live with mental illness (which is 1 in 5), that over 1 in 5 youths (ages 13-18) are currently living with some type of mental illness, and that 25% of US adults were living with a serious mental illness.

A probability study of 1218 Jamaicans and 2068 Guyanese people found that "Guyanese compared with Jamaicans for alcohol abuse (3.6% vs 2.2%), drug abuse (1.4% vs 1.3%), substance abuse (4.7% vs 2.7%) and mania (0.4% vs 0.1%). The rate of depression, however, was higher among Jamaicans than Guyanese (7.4% vs 4.1%)" (: Lacey, et al., 2016; p. 1). Based on Lacey and colleagues' study, there are disparities in the mental health conditions experienced between Jamaicans and Guyanese. A study by Gaviria and Rondon (2010) went further than the one conducted by Lacey, et al. (2016), which found it is that 9.8% of people in Latin America and the Caribbean suffer from depression, 11.3% from alcohol abuse, and 2.1% for drug abuse and dependence.

According to Kohn et al. (2018):

Data from community-based surveys of mental disorders in Argentina, Brazil, Canada, Chile, Colombia, Guatemala, Mexico, Peru, and the United States were utilized …found that Mental and substance use disorders accounted for 10.5% of the global burden of disease in the Americas. The 12-month prevalence rate of severe mental disorders ranged from 2% – 10% across studies. The weighted mean treatment gap in the Americas for moderate to severe disorders was 65.7%; North America, 53.2%; Latin America, 74.7%; Mesoamerica, 78.7%; and South America, 73.1%. The treatment gap for severe mental disorders in children and adolescents was over 50%. One-third of the indigenous population in the United States and 80% in Latin America had not received treatment. (p. 42)

The study by Kohn and colleagues emphasized that mental issues are typical across the globe including in developed nations. The English-speaking Caribbean has found that young people were living with mental health issues (Liverpool, et al., 2018), which speaks to the importance of examining mental health. Continuing, the literature also forwarded that eating disorders are a by-product of mental health issues (WHO, 2022b) and that dieting is associated with general health (Fadnes, et al., 2022; Harvard T.H. Chan School of Public Health, 2023; World Economic Forum, 2022).

Outside of eating disorders that play a significant role in determining mental health issues, an author forwarded that there are emerging some mental health challenges in the Caribbean. Hutchinson (2005) believed that suicidal behaviour, self-inflicted behaviours, substance abuse disorders, comorbidities, other psychiatric disorders, the burden of chronic diseases on psychiatric disorders, and increasing major crimes such as rape, homicide, robberies, sex with females under 16 years are some of the emerging mental health challenges for the Caribbean.

Mahy (2005) opined that small states in the Caribbean faced a different issue than those identified by Hutchinson (2005). He identified not having a mental health hospital and/or a psychiatric unit as well as a small percentage of trained mental health specialists to address some of the matters forwarded by Hutchinson as a serious problem for small Caribbean nations (Antigua/Barbuda, Dominica, Saint Lucia, St. Vincent and the Grenadine, Grenada, British Virgin Islands, Montserrat, and Anguilla). Mahy (2005) argued that the small island states in the

Caribbean depend on the big nations such as Jamaica, Trinidad and Tobago and the Bahamas for assistance in mental health care.

The literature shows that there is a relationship between mental health and social media usage (Braghieri, et al., 2022; Karim, et al. 2020; Seo, et al., 2023; Sidani, et al., 2020) and this was evident among young people (Berryman et al., 2018; Erevik, et al., 2021; Marwick & Boyd, 2014; Neira & Barber, 2014), how the small Caribbean nations fair in the future. The researcher extensively reviewed the literature and no study was found at the time of writing this book that examined social media usage and mental health challenges in small Caribbean islands, and this was the case for Jamaica. Is there any true association between social media usage and mental health? The matter of the association between social media usage and mental health is extensively reviewed in the next paragraph.

Mental Health and Social Media

According to Karim et al. (2020), "Because social media is a relatively new phenomenon, the potential links between their use and mental health have not been widely investigated" (p. e8627). Karim and colleagues made the previous statement in 2020, and a search of the literature does not concur with the perspective. A review of EBSCOhost in the library database of the Atlantic International University (AIU) found approximately 1,700 articles on social media and mental health. Social media have been found to reduce physical activity, which has been found to increase anxiety and depression among people (Martinsen, 2008). A study of young adults found that social media usage was not predictive in explaining impaired mental health functioning (Berryman, et al., 2018). However, Berryman and colleagues found that social media usage predicts suicidal ideation.

The social media usage and mental health phenomenon appear to be never-ending and foster the need for more research in the area. Marwick & Boyd (2014) opined, "A previous study found no relationship between the amount of time spent on social media and depression or between social media-related activities, such as the number of online friends and the number of "selfies", and depression [p. 29]. This is yet another side to the social media usage and mental health discourse. However, Neira & Barber (2014) "found that while higher investment in social media (e.g. active social media use) predicted adolescents' depressive symptoms, no relationship was found between the frequency of social media use and depressed mood [p. 28]. Erevik et al. (2021) found a relationship between social media usage and mental health, with no contradiction to this fact.

There was at least one study that found a positive association between social media usage and mental health (Seo, et al., 2023). Seo et al. (2023) wrote, "Those who use social media primarily for networking purposes reported better mental health, whereas social media use for information seeking was not significantly associated with their mental health" (p. 1). One of the deductions that can be made from Seo and colleagues' work is that social media usage has some negative effects on the mental health of people. Braghieri et al. (2022) conducted a quasi-experiment on social media usage and mental health and had some interesting findings compared to the many survey research findings on the topic.

> We provide quasi-experimental estimates of the impact of social media on mental health by leveraging a unique natural experiment: the staggered introduction of Facebook across US colleges. Our analysis couples data on student mental health around the years of Facebook's expansion with a generalized difference-in-differences empirical strategy. We find that the rollout of Facebook at a college hurt students' mental health. It also

increased the likelihood with which students reported experiencing impairments to academic performance due to poor mental health" (Braghieri et al. (2022; p. 3660). Although Braghieri et al.'s (2022) work was limited to Facebook and as such is not generalizable to social media use, it provides some insights into the phenomenon from a non-survey research perspective. Social media usage influences the mental health and academic performance of college students. Social media usage is not only influencing the mental health status of students; but, there is evidence that it affects the mental health status of parents. Sidani et al. (2020) found that a one per cent increase in parental social media usage was associated with 51% greater odds of experiencing depressive symptoms.

The literature is inconclusive on the relationship between social media usage and mental health status. Based on the various studies, the difference in findings may be due to the population and sub-topics as well as the assessment tool of mental health. Another issue in the discourse is gender, hence this book brings in gender in the health discussion.

Gender

The World Health Organization (2005) forwarded a position that there is a disparity between contracting many diseases and the gender constitution of an individual. One health psychologist, Phillip Rice, in concurring with WHO, argued that differences in death and illnesses are the result of differential risks acquired from functions, stress, lifestyles and 'preventative health practices' (Rice 1998).

Biomedical studies showed that there are gender-specific diseases. The examples here are prostate cancer (which affects only men) and cervical cancer (plague only women). Rice believed that this health difference between the sexes is due to social support. According to Rice (1998), Rodin and Ickovics (1990) this can be explained by epidemiological trends.

Lifestyle practices may justify the advantages that women enjoy compared to men concerning health status. However, a survey done by Rudkin found that women have lower levels of well-being (i.e. economic) than men (Rudkin 1993 222). This finding is further sanctioned by Haveman et al (2003) whose study revealed that retired men's well-being was higher than that of their female counterparts because men usually received more material resources, and more retired benefits compared to women ages 65 years and older. Thus with men receiving more than women, and having a more durable possession than women, their material well-being is higher in later life.

The issue extends beyond those two types of chronic illnesses as Courtenay (2003) noted from research conducted by the Department of Health and Human Services (2000) and Centers for Disease Control (1997) that from the 15 leading causes of death except Alzheimer's disease, the death rates are higher for men and boys in all age cohorts compared to women and girls. Embedded within this theorizing are the differences in fatal diseases that are explained by gender constitution (Seltzer and Hendricks 1989, 7), which Courtenay (2003) explained are due to behavioural practices of the sexes and goes to explain the fact that men are dying 6 years earlier than females (U.S. Preventive Services Task Force, 1996).

Females, on the other hand, have a higher propensity than males to contract particular conditions such as depression, osteoporosis and osteoarthritis (W.H.O 2005, p.14; Herzog 1989, p.36). Herzog (1989) noted that "…it appears that older women are more likely to be impaired by their health problems, while older men are more likely to die from them." A study that was conducted by Schoen et al. (1998) on a group of adolescents reveals something different from that which was reported by WHO. They found that males are more likely than females to feel stressed and 'overwhelmed' or 'depressed', and they attributed this to the limitedness of men's social networks.

Other research has agreed with Schoen et al that men in general tend to be more stressed and less healthy than females and further argued that men can use denial, distraction, alcoholism and other social strategies to conceal their illness or disabilities (Friedman, 1992; Kopp, Shrabski, and Szedmak, 1998; Weidner and Collins, 1993; Sutkin and Good, 1987). On the other hand, Herzog (1989) in *Physical and Mental Health in Older Women*, using studies from several experts wrote that females had higher rates of depression than their male counterparts. Could suicide be used as a proxy for depression? Suicide is taken from death registers, which is likely to be underreported for the aged, since other illnesses are present, and may be substituted as the cause of mortality (Herzog 1989). Herzog noted that data on suicide and depression yielded different results, and based on this fact, suicide cannot be used as an indicator of depression.

Males, nevertheless, are more likely to have heart diseases, gout and high blood pressure than women are. WHO attributes this biomedical condition to differences between the genders based on hormonal differentiation, social networks and support, and cultural and lifestyle practices of the sexes, which was concurred by Courtenay et al. (2002).

Based on the demographic model from abridged Life Tables, mortality is different between the genders (Elo 2001; Bourne, 2009f). Generally, from the United Nations statistical databases, life expectancy for males is lower than for females. This is particularly true for females in the old-aged cohorts (United Nations 2004; Moore et al. 1997). Moore et al. (1997) added, "Females' life expectancies are likely to remain above that for males [Elo 2001] for the foreseeable future, among both the population as a whole and the elderly" (Moore et al. 1997, 12). Among the justifications for the differential in life expectancy, the sexes are linked with the health consciousness of women and their approach to preventative care. Unlike women, worldwide men have a reluctance to 'seek health care' compared to their female counterparts. It follows in truth that women have bought themselves additional years in their younger years, and it is a practice that they continue throughout their lifetime which makes the gap in age differential what it is – which is approximately a 4-year difference in Jamaica.

Elo (2001,106) in his discussion of the findings from the use of the vital registration and the census data set forwarded reduction in infant mortality and sex-specific mortality favoured women and accounted for the disparity in life expectancy between the sexes. Within the workings of this space, demographers assume that we are in the third stage of the epidemiological transition (Omran 1971) in which health conditions associated with chronic conditions have replaced infectious and parasitic illness as the dominant cause of death.

Studies have revealed that the classification of many diseases affects a particular gender. In that, for particular chronic viruses, the primary contributor to death is ischemic heart diseases that substantially are a man's rather than a woman's disease. In research conducted jointly by the University of Michigan in the United States and the Bureau of Health Promotion in Taiwan on elderly Taiwanese, between 1989 and 1993, of 4,049 people of 60 years and beyond, several socio-economic determinants were studied concerning mortality. From the findings, age is positively related to health conditions, with females, married people, primary level education and post-primary level graduands negatively related to health conditions (Zimmer, Martin and Lin 2003, p.17).

Embedded within Zimmer, Martin and Lin's findings is the direct relationship between ageing and health conditions compared to an inverse relationship that exists between health conditions and females, primary and post-primary level graduands and married people. It is clear from the included socio-economic factors mentioned previously that males who are older than sixty years have a higher propensity to be ill than females. Health conditions, therefore, are influenced by marital status (i.e. married people). This reality represents a situation, where married people are less likely to have particular health conditions than those who are in common-law, visiting relationships or single. A noteworthy finding is the direct relationship between poverty and health conditions. Embedded within this socio-physical situation is the difficulty of the poor to seek and afford proper preventive care in comparison to the rich or those in the middle class, therefore making them vulnerable to poor health conditions.

From the various studies presented, within the socio-demographic reality of longer life for females, there is a paradox in that living longer implies that there is a higher probability of preventative and curative costs of care. It should be noted here that a study conducted by Franzini et al. (2004) on native Mexicans in Texas found that females had worse mental and self-reported health than their male counterparts did, but not physical health. Franzine et al's work contravenes many findings on gender and health status. Another study on *socioeconomic determinants of mortality in two Canadian provinces* found that household income and education were significant in predicting mortality. When gender was introduced within the model, the association dissipated (Roos et al. 2004).

A study conducted by McDonough and Walters (2001) revealed that women had a 23 per cent higher distress score than men and were more likely to report chronic diseases compared to males (30%). It was found that men believed their health was better (2% higher) than that self-reported by females. McDonough and Walters used data from a longitudinal study named the Canadian National Population Health Survey (NPHS). The study was initiated in 1994, and data were collected every second year for six years. The information was taken from 20,000 household members who were 12 years and older.

Research carried out by a group of economists (Headey and Wooden, 2004) revealed that "...women are slightly more likely to report higher levels of life satisfaction than men (mean=78.3, compared with 77.1 for men..." (Headey and Wooden 2004, 14). Based on the nature of the study, '...subjective well-being and ill-being', the reported well-being (measured by life satisfaction) of women is higher than that of men but males have higher financial well-being than females (Headey and Wooden 2004, 16). The gender and health phenomenon is crucial to the health discourse and even the World Health Organization (2023a) wrote on the matter, which takes the discussion to general and mental health.

Gender and Psychological Well-being/Mental Health Status

The relationship between gender and health or age and health is documented in the literature, which dates back to the Bills of Mortality in 1665 (Boyce, N. (2020). Using self-reported health status or subjective well-being, starting with Grossman (1972), many studies established the quantitative relationship between health and age and health and ageing (Smith & Kington, 1997a, 1997b; Hambleton et al., 2005). Psychological well-being is a component of health/well-being and psychological well-being has been widely promulgated as a measure of mental health (Ryff's Psychological Well-Being Scales). Psychological well-being and mental health are used synonymously in some studies. Matud et al. (2019) opined, "Men's well-being also was higher in professional men and in men with a skilled non-manual occupation, men with high femininity and men who were not single, divorced or widowed." (p. 1). This supports the literature that there is a gender gap in mental health status (Pattyn, et al., 2015).

The gender mental health gap may be explained by the healthcare-seeking behaviour of the sexes. Pattyn et al.'s (2015) perspective on gender healthcare-seeking behaviour offers some insight into the mental health results found in Matud et al.'s (2019) work. According to Pattyn et al. (2015), "The gender gap in mental health service use is due not only to men and their negative attitudes toward help-seeking but also to structured social norms that are reconstructed in interactions (p 1089). Pattyn et al. (2015) attributed the gender gap in mental health status to the culture, which concurs with the work of Rosenfield & Smith (2009) and was also established in an epidemiological study (Seedat, et al., 2009).

Biological Age and Well-being

Organisms age naturally, which explains biological ageing. This approach emphasizes the longevity of the cells, about the number of years the organism can live. Thus, in this construction, the human body (an organism) is valued based on the physical appearance and/or state of the cells. Embedded in this apparatus is the genetic composition of the survivor. This occurs where the body's longevity is explained by genetic components (See for example Yashin & Iachine 1997, 32). Gompertz's law in Gavriolov and Gavrilova (2001) shows that there is a fundamental quantitative theory of ageing and mortality of certain species (the examples here are as follows – humans, human lice, rats mice, fruit flies, and flour beetles (see also, Gavriolov & Gavrilova 1991). Gompertz's law went further to establish that human mortality increases twofold with every 8 years of an adult life, which means that ageing increases in geometric progression. This phenomenon means that human mortality increases with the age of the human adult, but that this becomes less progress in advanced ageing. Thus, biological ageing is a process where the human cells degenerate with years (i.e. the cells die with increasing age), which is explored in evolutionary biology (see Medawar 1946; Bourne, 2009f; Carnes and Olshansky 1993; Carnes et al. 1999; Charlesworth 1994). However, studies have shown that using evolutionary theory for "late-life mortality plateaus", fails because of the arguably unrealistic set of assumptions that the theory uses to establish itself (Mueller & Rose 1996; Charlesworth & Partridge 1997; Pletcher & Curtsinger 1998; Wachter 1999).

Reliability theory, on the other hand, is a better-fitted explanation for the ageing of humans than that argued by Gompertz's law as the 'failing law' speaks to the deterioration of human organisms with age (Gavrilov & Gavrilova 2001) as well as non-ageing term. The latter based on Gavrilov and Gavrilova (2001) can occur because of accidents and acute infection, which are called "extrinsic causes of death. While Gompertz's law speaks to mortality in ageing organisms due to age-related degenerative illnesses such as heart diseases and cancers, part of the reliability function is Gompertz's function as well as the non-ageing component.

When the biological approach is used to measure ageing, this may be problematic as two different individuals with the same organs and physical appearance may not be able to perform at the same rates, which speaks to the difficulty in using this construct in measuring ageing. Nevertheless, this construct can compare and contrast organisms for several years, and a cell may be likely to exist. Erber (2005), argues that this is undoubtedly subjective, as we are unable within definiteness predict the life span of a living cell (Erber, 2005, p. 9).

Interestingly, the biological approach highlights that the ageing process comes with changes in physical functioning. The oldest-old categorization is said to have the least physical functioning compared to the other classifications in chronological ageing. The young-old, on the other hand, are more likely to be the most functioning as the organism is just beginning the transition into the aged arena (see for example Bourne, 2009f; Brannon & Fiest, 2004; Erber, 2005).

To avoid such pitfalls in constructions that may arise with the use of the biological approach, ergo, for all intent and purposes, given the nature of policy implications in effective planning, the researcher is forwarding the perspective that seniority in age commences at age 65 years – using the chronological ageing approach.

The ageing transition, both chronological and biological ageing has a similar tenet. In that, as we move from young-old to oldest-old, the body deteriorates and what was of low severity in the earlier part of the ageing process becomes of critical mass in the latter stage. Hence, at the introductory stage of the ageing transition, the individual may feel the same as when he/she was in the working-age population, but the reality is the body is in a declining mode. Because humans are continuously operating with negatives and positives, as he/she becomes older – using the ageing transition (i.e. 65 years and older) – the losses (or negatives) outweigh the positives. This simply means that the functionality limitation of the body falls, and so opens the person to a higher probability of becoming susceptible to morbidity and mortality. Secondly, the environment, which may not have been problematic in the past, now becomes a health hazard. One University of Chicago scholar summarizes this quite well in Table 1.

Table 1

Characteristics of the Three Categories of Elderly, and the Ageing Transition

Characteristic	**The Ageing Transition**		
	Young-old	Aged[1]	Oldest-Old
Health problems	Low	Moderate	High
Physical disability	Low	Moderate	High
Demand for medical care	Low	Moderate	High
Demand for public service	Low	Moderate	High
Demands on children	Low	Moderate	High
Dependency on other	Low	Moderate	High
Social isolation	Low	Moderate	High

Source: This is taken from *Essays in Human Ecology* 4. Bogue (1999, p. 3).
[1] Donald Bogue (1999) used aged (age 75 – 84 years) to refer to what this paper calls old-old

Age and Psychological Well-being/Mental Health Status

The literature established that there is a statistical association between subjective well-being and age (Biermann, et al., 2022; Diener & Suh, 1998; Hambleton, et al., 2005; Horley & Lavery, 1995; Shmotkin, 1990; Stone, et al., 2020; Xing & Huang, 2014), objective well-being and age (Bogue, 1999; Bourne, 2009f; Statistics Canada, 2015; Western & Tomaszewski, 2016), and general well-being and age (Bourne, 2008a, 2008b; Bourne & McGrowder, 2010a; Smith & Kington, 1997a, 1997b;). There is a consensus in the literature that the association between age and health (subjective and objective) is a negative one. Is the relationship between general good health (health) or subjective health (well-being) or objective health (life expectancy) the same for psychological well-being? Psychological well-being (mental health) is a component of general well-being or health; but is it correct to extrapolate that what appears for age and general health, will be the same for psychological well-being?

The negative relationship that exists between age and general subjective well-being is the same between age and psychological well-being. Many studies quantitatively established the inverse relationship between age and psychological well-being (López et al., 2020; Steptoe, et al., 2015; Yeung, 2017). Some studies found a complex relationship between ageing and psychological well-being. Blanchflower and Oswald (2008) and Weiss, et al. (2012) found a curvilinear relationship between age and psychological well-being. It can be extrapolated from curvilinear studies that the relationship between ageing and psychological well-being is not stationary over the lifespan of the individual, which explains the U-shaped relationship. Stone et al. (2010), on the other hand, contradict the U-shaped relationship between age and psychological well-being.

When mental health is brought into the discourse, are the findings different from those obtained for general health and age, and subjective well-being and age, and psychological well-being and age? According to the Division of Population Health, National Center for Chronic Disease Prevention and Health Promotion (2023), "As people age, they may experience certain life changes that impact their mental health, such as coping with a serious illness or losing a loved one. Although many people will adjust to these life changes, some may experience feelings of grief, social isolation, or loneliness. When these feelings persist, they can lead to mental illnesses, such as depression and anxiety." The perspective of the National Center for Chronic Disease Prevention and Health Promotion implies that the relationship between mental health and ageing is not a simple one-directional one. This idea is congruent with the curvilinear relationship found by Blanchflower and Oswald (2008) and Weiss, et al. (2012). Furthermore, when illnesses appear and there are many other illnesses arising that were not present at younger ages, the relationship between ageing and mental health decreases. This reality explains the inverse relationship found between mental and ageing (see, Chen, et al., 2022; National Institute of Mental Health, 2023; WHO, 2023). Using meta-analysis, Solmi et al. (2022) found that good mental health declines with age and ageing as well as an increase in ageing and mental health disorders such as phobias, anxiety, and attention deficit hyperactivity disorder (see also Cybulski, et al., 2017; WHO, 2023b).

CHAPTER 4

RESEARCH METHODS

Chapter 4 provides a detailed description of the methods and materials used to provide answers to the current research questions. This book employed a quantitative cross-sectional design. The quantitative perspective is survey research. The survey research was a web-based non-probability sampling cross-sectional descriptive research design (Babbie, 2010; Polit, 1996; Powell *et al.*, 2007; Rea & Parker, 2005; Neuman, 2014). The researcher utilized a standardized instrument to collect data from Jamaica by way of the Psychological Well-being Questionnaire developed by Ryff; items on social media platforms used, frequency of social media usage, and selected demographic variables.

The data was collected over approximately four-to-six weeks. For the survey research, the instrument was designed using textbooks on survey research and designing surveys (Powell *et al.*, 2007; Rea and Parker, 2005), and the process was in keeping with the research objectives.

This study sought and protected the identity of the respondents by 1. not using any personal identifier except age group, members, educational attainment, area of residence, and nationality, 2. informing respondents that they may withdraw at any time during the process and return their questionnaire without any form of penalization or repercussion (Appendix 1), and 3. collecting the data by way of the internet. The standard instrument was designed and uploaded to Survey Monkey. The sample was a purposive one. For the qualitative perspective of the study, the research team employed snowballing to ascertain the participants.

The respondent's consent was based on the completion and submission of the instrument. The researcher examined the IP addresses to ensure that an instrument was completed by only one person. If there were more than one of the same IP addresses, the researcher would allow the first one to remain and delete the second IP address.

A paid Survey Monkey account was used, which allows for the collection of web-based data and the provision of the Statistical Package for the Social Sciences (SPSS) database. The research team downloaded the quantitative data to the SPSS database, where analyses facilitate the answers to the various research questions and objectives using descriptive statistics and percentages (Bryman & Cramer, 2011; Polit, 1996). The findings, therefore, were displayed using graphs and tables. Cross-tabulations to examine the bivariate analyses of non-metric variables (i.e., nominal and ordinal)- (Bourne, 2009g; Bryman & Cramer, 2011; Polit, 1996). A p-value of 5 per cent determined the level of significance in a two-tailed test.

The researchers addressed the treatment of missing data in the current study by reviewing the extensive work on missing data to ensure alignment with recommended best practices (Bodner, 2008; Graham, 2009; Kang, 2013; Little et al., 2012); there is no consensus on a rule of thumb on the matter. Hence, the researcher opted to employ two guidelines. These were 1. in the event more than 30% of the data is missing, the variable from analysis, and 2. where there are less than 30% of missing cases, the system missing in the SPSS program was used to assign a value for those cases (Bourne, 2009g).

THE STUDY POPULATION AND SAMPLE

The respondents for this book consisted of resident Jamaicans who live in one of the fourteen parishes in Jamaica. Figure 5 provides a map of Jamaica and Table 1 gives a detailed description of the human population of Jamaica disaggregated by parish for the latest published time (2018; STATIN, 2023).

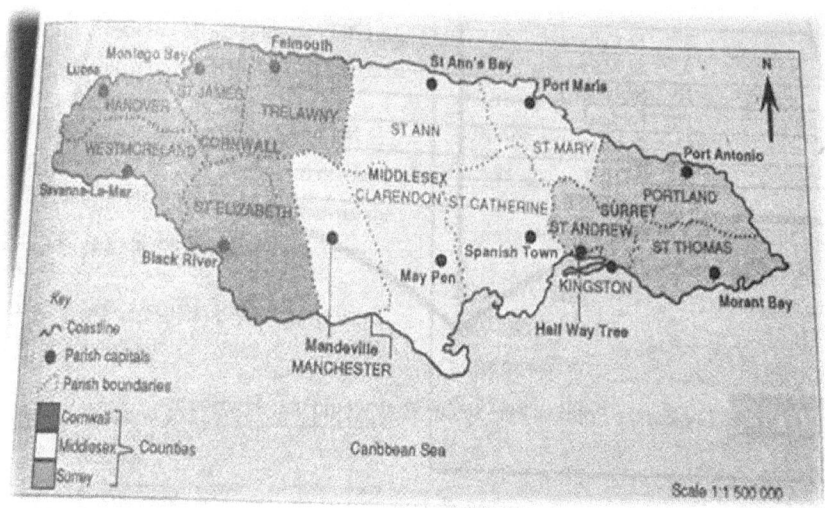

Figure 5. Map of 3 counties in Jamaica.
Note. Reprinted from: http://www.electionpassport.com/files/JM-Counties.gif

The sample size was computed based on a 1) population of 2,727,503 resident Jamaicans, 2) a 95% confidence interval, and 3) a 3% margin of error (Babbie, 2010; Hair, Black, Babin, et al., 2018; Neuman, 2014). Using the previously mentioned figures, the Survey Monkey calculator computed a sample size of 1,067 Jamaicans across the fourteen parishes. The researcher disaggregated the 1,067 Jamaicans in the sample based on the same percentage as that of the population (Table 2).

Table 2

Human Population and Sample of Jamaica

Parish	Human Population, 2018	% Population[1]	Human Sample[1]	% Human Sample[1]
Kingston and St Andrew	669,978	24.6	262	24.6
St Thomas	94,968	3.5	37	3.5
Portland	82,669	3.0	32	3.0
St Mary	114,902	4.2	45	4.2
St Ann	174,256	6.4	68	6.4
Trelawny	76,005	2.8	30	2.8
St James	185,753	6.8	73	6.8
Hanover	70,287	2.6	27	2.6
Westmoreland	145,673	5.3	57	5.3
St Elizabeth	151,885	5.6	59	5.6
Manchester	191,940	7.0	75	7.0
Clarendon	247,778	9.1	97	9.1
St Catherine	521,409	19.1	204	19.1
Total	2,727,503	100.0	1067	100.0

Source: Statistical Institute of Jamaica (2023)
[1] The figure was computed by Paul Andrew Bourne

INCLUSION CRITERIA

There are two criteria for inclusion in the current study. The two inclusions are as follows: 1. 18+ years old, and 2. Resident Jamaican. The age condition was simple to remove the need for parent/guardian consent from the respondents. The legal age in Jamaica is 18 years, and so the researcher used this age because people can provide their consent.

EXCLUSION CRITERIA

People were excluded from this study based on 1. Being less than 18 years old at the time of the survey, 2. Medically impaired, 3. In hospital or prison, 4. non-Jamaicans, 5. Non-resident Jamaican at the time of the survey, and 6. Not having a cellular phone.

CONCEPTUALIZATION AND OPERATIONALIZATION OF VARIABLES

Conceptualization

Age: The number of years lived by a person as of his/her last birthday.

Gender: For this book, the World Health Organization's (WHO) definition of gender is used. The WHO opined, "Gender refers to the characteristics of women, men, girls and boys that are socially constructed. This includes norms, behaviours and roles associated with being a woman, man, girl or boy, as well as relationships with each other. As a social construct, gender varies from society to society and can change over time".

Mental health: According to the World Health Organization (WHO), "Mental health is a state of mental well-being that enables people to cope with the stresses of life, realize their abilities, learn well and work well, and contribute to their community. It is an integral component of health and well-being that underpins our individual and collective abilities to make decisions, build relationships and shape the world we live in" (WHO, 2022a). This book uses the conceptualization of the WHO on mental health.

Social Media: Jones's (2023) definition of social media is used in this book. Jones opined, "Social media is understood as the different forms of online communication used by people to create networks, communities, and collectives to share information, ideas, messages, and other content, such as videos."

Psychological well-being: Psychological well-being is the core feature of mental health (Tang, et al., 2019). Dhanabhakyam & Sarath (2023) postulated, "Psychological well-being is a multifaceted and multidimensional construct that encompasses an individual's overall happiness, satisfaction with life, and mental and emotional health" (p. 603). Psychological well-being is widely used and validated in the literature to measure mental health and is equally extended to assess well-being (Abbott, et al., 206; Burns, 2016; Ryff & Keyes, 1995; Ryff & Singer, 2006; Ryff, 1989a, 1989b, 1989c; Seifert, 2005; Springer & Hauser, 2006; Springer, et al., 2006).

Operationalization

Age is classed into three groups. These are 1. Young people adults (18-29 years), 2. Middle-aged adults (30-59 years), and 3. Elderly (60+ years).

Psychological well-being. Ryff's 18-item scale was used to assess this concept. The item options ranged from 1 = strongly agree; 2 = somewhat agree; 3 = a little agree; 4 = neither, agree or disagree; 5 = a little disagree; 6 = somewhat disagree; 7 = strongly disagree. The researcher sought and obtained permission to use the instrument for usage in this book (Appendix 4).

Instrumentation

A self -self-administered questionnaire (Appendix 5) was used to assess the variables. Questionnaires consist of two sections with a total of 41 items. Items 1 to 16 assess the psychological well-being of Jamaicans, 17 to 39 deal with social media networks and usage, and 40 to 43 deal with demographic variables such as age, gender, and nationality as well as whether the individual currently resides in Jamaica. The study variables, knowledge, practice and attitude were measured using 36 items. The first 16 items were used to assess psychological well-being. The scoring of the first 16 items was based on the Autonomy subscale items Q15, Q17, and Q18. The Environmental Mastery subscale items are Q4, Q8, Q9. The Personal Growth subscale items are Q11, Q12, Q14. The Positive Relations with Others subscale items are Q6, Q13, Q16. The Purpose in Life

subscale items are Q3, Q7, Q10. The Self-Acceptance subscale items are Q1, Q2, and Q5. Additionally, Q1, Q2, Q3, Q8, Q9, Q11, Q12, Q13, Q17, and Q18 were reverse-scored. Reverse-scored items are worded in the opposite direction of what the scale is measuring. The formula for reverse-scoring an item is:

((Number of scale points) + 1) - (Respondent's answer)

For example, Q1 is a 7-point scale. If a respondent answered 3 on Q1, there is a re-code of their answer as: $(7 + 1) - 3 = 5$.

In other words, a 5 is entered for this respondent's answer to Q1.

To calculate subscale scores for each participant, sum respondents' answers to each subscale's items. Higher scores mean higher levels of psychological well-being.

Data Collection

Approval was sought from the Department of Ethics at Atlantic International University (AIU). The data collection technique that was used is the web-based standardized questionnaire. The researcher used Survey Monkey and a written questionnaire to collect the information from prospective respondents. A standardized instrument was designed, and placed in Survey Monkey, and was distributed to prospective sampled respondents across the 14 parishes of Jamaica. After receiving approval, the researcher provided the participants with the questionnaires accompanied by an explanation of the study (via Survey Monkey). Assurance of confidentiality and anonymity was upheld by not including any personal identifier on the instrument. The survey was forwarded to respondents' mobile phones or emails. Data collection was carried out over at most four weeks.

RELIABILITY AND VALIDITY

Researchers have argued that validation and verification are important issues in scientific research (Kuhn, 1996; Balashov and Rosenberg, 2002), and offer an insight into the science of the study. For research to be credible, reliability and validity must be established and employed in the research process (Babbie, 2010; Creswell, 2014). Babbie (2010) and Neuman (2014) believed that reliability is concerned with the internal consistency of the methods, conditions and results while validity deals with the accurate interpretability of the results and the generalizability of the results.

RELIABILITY

Reliability speaks to the probability that the scale items perform their intended function adequately based on the specified period. Hence, the researcher examined the reliability of the Psychological Well-Being Scale by way of Cronbach's alpha. The general rule of thumb for a good Cronbach is a value of at least 70% (Tavakol, M., & Dennick, R. (2011), which would measure a good internal consistency of the scale or test items (Cronbach, 1951).

VALIDITY

For this study, the two types of validity that were examined included: 1. Content and 2. Construct validity. Content validity addresses the extent to which the scale (or items) fairly represents the entire domain of test items (Anastasia, 1988; Hair, et al., 2018; Rusticus, 2014; Salkind, 2010). Rusticus (2014) argued that "There are three key aspects of content validity: domain definition, domain representation, and domain relevance" (p. 1). Factor analysis is used to determine content validity (Izquierdo, Olea, & Abad, F. 2014; Watkins, 2018) by way of The Screeplot, Eigenvalues (which should be at least 1), and KMO and Bartlett's Test (Bartlett, 1951, 1954; Hair et al., 2018; Kaiser, 1958, 1974; Watkins, 2018).

Construct validity, on the other hand, is the extent to which the measure behaves consistently to the theoretical hypothesis or other internal reliability analysis. Like content validity, factor analysis is used to determine construct validity.

DATA ANALYSIS

For this survey instrument (self-administered standardized questionnaire), the large volume of data was stored, retrieved and analyzed using the Statistical Packages for the Social Sciences (SPSS) for Windows version 27.0 (SPSS Inc; Chicago, IL, USA). Descriptive statistics were performed on the data as well as percentage and frequency distributions. Descriptive statistics allowed the researcher to meaningfully describe the many pieces of data collected Gay, Mills, & Airasian (2009). Statistical significance determined a p-value less than or equal to five percentage points (≤ 0.05) – two-tailed. In addition to descriptive statistics, scatter plots and box plots were also used to analyze the data. The researcher also performed χ^2 tests to compare associations in non-metric variables and Independent sample-t tests (Gay et al., 2009; Polit, 1996). Box plots were used to display a graphic presentation of categorizations of a non-metric variable on a metric variable.

For the Likert scale questions (i.e., 1-16), the researcher employed the scoring design as outlined by Ryff. Following the previous computations, the researcher conducted a factor analysis on the Psychological Well-being Scale, descriptive statistics bivariate Analysis, and multivariate analysis to create the final model.

ETHICAL ISSUES

Ethical clearance was solicited from the ethics committees of the Atlantic International University (AIU; Appendix 2). Before the researcher began this book, he did a few training in ethics (Appendix 3). All the respondents were required to give their consent before being included in the study. Respondents were informed of the study, their roles and duties as well as the right to withdraw at any time if the need arises. The consent form outlined the rights and approach in the overall research process, and no personal identifiers were placed on the questionnaire. All the participants were required to give their consent before being included in the study (See Appendix 1). The researcher sought approval from these institutions before the questionnaires were issued.

CHAPTER 5

Findings and Interpretations

Introduction

This book seeks to examine whether social media usage among Jamaicans influences their mental health status. This chapter (chapter 4) begins with a demographic table, which presents the basic characteristics of the sampled respondents. The demographic characteristic is followed by issues on social media usage, testing the psychometric properties of the 18-item Ryff's Psychological Well-being Scale (PWBS), descriptive statistics on PWBS, the multiple linear regression analysis of the selected variables and whether they influence PWBS or mental health status. The chapter closes off with a summative paragraph.

Demographic Characteristics of the Sampled Respondents

Table 1 presents the demographic characteristics of the sampled respondents. There are 587 respondents for this book. Of the 587 respondents, the majority were adults (75.3%, n=442), all were Jamaicans, and 97.8% were currently on the Island or residence Jamaicans.

Table 1
Demographic Characteristics of the Sampled Respondents, n= 587

Details	% (N)
Age cohort	
Youth	22.3 (131)
Adults	75.3 (442)
Seniors	2.4 (14)
Gender	
Female	42.3 (96)
Male	57.7 (131)

Jamaican	100.0 (587)
Currently resides in Jamaica	
On the Island	97.8 (574)
Off the Island	2.2 (13)

Table 2 presents issues on social media networking of the sampled respondents. Eight-seven out of every 100 of the sampled respondents had an active social media account with the majority of the sample on average spending less than 5 hours on social media (67.5%).

Table 2
Issues on Social Media Networking, N=587

Details	% (n)
Active Social Media Network Account	
No	12.6 (74)
Yes	87.4 (513)
Daily Time Spent on Social Media Networks	
0 – 4 hours	67.5 (394)
5 – 9 hours	25,2 (147)
10 – 14 hours	4.4 (26)
15 – 19 hours	1.7 (10)
20 – 24 hours	1.2 (7)
Type of Social Media Account Used	
Facebook	74.8
Instagram	99.5
Youtube	30.1

LinkedIn	95.4
WhatsApp	76.7
Tik Tok	35.1
Twitter	6.2
Reddit	42.6
Snapchat	34.1
Quora	68.0
Digg	10.6
Pinterest	0.8
Fancy	1.0
Polyvore	0.4
Etsy	23.0
Tumblr	6.2
WordPress	1.7
Tumblr	0.8
Zinati	5.2
TripAdvisor	0.4

Table 3 presents an analysis of variance for the average daily number of hours spent on social media by age cohort. On average, youth spent 8 hours ± 5 hours on social media daily compared to 4 hours ± 3 hours for adults and 2.4 hours ± 2 for seniors (i.e., 65+ years).

Table 3
Analysis of Variance

Details	Average Daily Number of Hours spent on Social Media
Age cohort[1]	Mean±Standard deviation; 95%CI
Youth	5.7± 4.7; 4.5 - 6.82
Adults	3.5±3.0; 3.2 - 3.8
Seniors	2.4±1.7; 0.97 - 3.8

[1]$F[2,437] = 142.104$, p-value < 0.001

Confirmatory Factor Analysis

Factor analysis is a statistical tool that is used in examining the psychometric properties of a scale or scale building (Bartlett, 1950, 1954, 1960; Brillinger, et al., 2004; Hair, et al. 2018; Kaiser, 1960, 1970, 1974; Tabachnick & Fidell, 2007). The statistical technique of factor analysis allows for the quantitative assessment of the suitability and appropriateness of scale to measure the intended phenomenon. Ryff Psychological Well-being Scale was developed to evaluate the psychological state of people, and it has been tested and re-tested by many scholars (Ryff, 1989a, 1989b, 1989c; Ryff & Keyes, 1995; Ryff & Singer, 2006; Springer & Hauser, 2006; Seifert, 2005).

There are three versions of the Ryff Psychological Well-being Scale: 1. Short-version (18 items), 2. medium version (19-to-53 items) and 3. the long-version (54 items). The short version has been widely used to assess psychological or the mental health status of different populations (Ryff, et al., 2010; Ryff & Keyes, 1995). This book examines the psychometric properties of the scale as developed by Ryff, and it is quantitatively validated for suitability and appropriateness before usage.

For the book, the researcher entered, stored, and retrieved the data from the Statistical Package for the Social Sciences, Version 28 for Windows. Before, the psychometric properties assessment, the researcher examines the data to validate whether the assumptions of factor analysis were upheld. The two assumptions of factor analysis are normality and the descriptive statistics for each item being more than 3.

Before performing Principal Component Analysis (PCA), the researcher examined the two main assumptions of factor analysis. Table 4 presents the descriptive statistics for the 7-point Likert scale for the Ryff Psychological Well-being Scale, the Short Version. The mean values range from 3.95 to 6.72. Based on the mean value for each of the 18 items, all the items meet this assumption of factor analysis.

Table 4

Descriptive Item Statistics for 18-Item Ryff Psychological Well-being Scale

Details			
	Mean	Std. Deviation	N
I like most parts of my personality	6.53	.986	469
When I look at the story of my life, I am pleased with how things have turned out so far	5.99	1.337	469
Some people wander through life, but I am not one of them	6.19	1.445	469
The demands of everyday life often get me down	3.97	2.091	469
"In many ways, I feel disappointed about my achievements in life."	4.95	2.160	469

Maintaining close relationships has been difficult and frustrating for me	4.81	2.251	469
I live life one day at a time and don't think about the future	5.34	1.989	469
In general, I feel I am in charge of the situation in which I live	5.74	1.630	469
I am good at managing the responsibilities of daily life	6.18	1.218	469
I sometimes feel as if I've done all there is to do in life	5.21	2.023	469
For me, life has been a continuous process of learning, changing, and growth	6.72	.818	469
I think it is important to have new experiences that challenge how I think about myself and the world	6.52	1.061	469
People would describe me as a giving person, willing to share my time with others	6.35	1.045	469
I gave up trying to make big improvements or changes in my life a long time ago	5.95	1.730	469
I tend to be influenced by people with strong opinions"	4.77	2.117	469
I have not experienced many warm and trusting relationships with others	4.52	2.204	469
"I have confidence in my own opinions, even if they are different from the way most other people think	6.44	1.046	469
I judge myself by what I think is important, not by the values of what others think is important	6.17	1.373	469

The issue of normality of 18 items was examined, and the results are presented in Table 5. Table 5 presents the Kolmogorov-Smirnov and Shapiro-Wilk test of normality. All 18 items met the assumption of normal distribution. Ryff Psychological Well-being Scale meets two assumptions for the usage of factor analysis by way of the Principal Component Analysis (PCA).

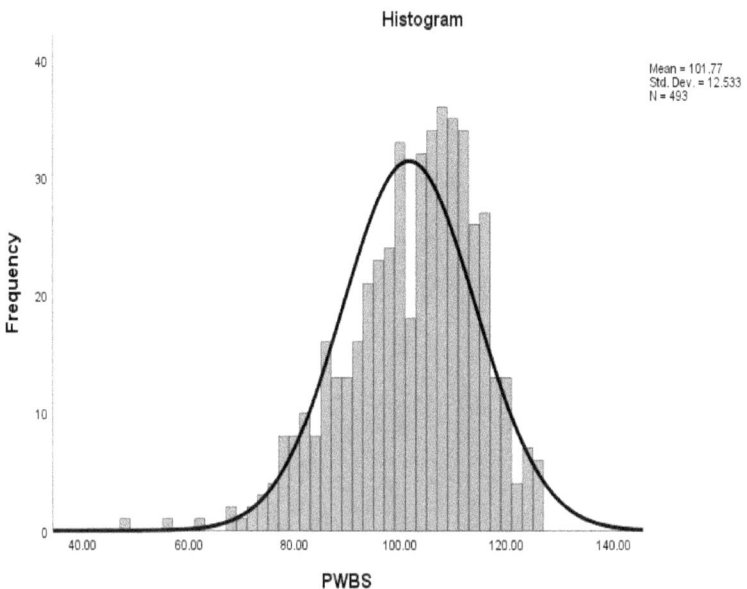

Figure A: Frequency Distribution Polygon of Ryff Psychological Well-being Scale

Figure A is a frequency polygon with a superimposed curve on the frequency polygons. The distribution is relatively normal as the skewness valuation was -0.61. For this book the acceptable skewness is less than 0.7, which means that values below the acceptable number indicate relative normality.

The phase in the preliminary inquiry was the internal reliability of the items, and this was assessed by way of Cronbach alpha. The Cronbach alpha for the 18-item Ryff Psychological Well-being Scale (PWBS) was 0.703. A value of at least 0.7 or 70% indicates that the 18-item scale is suitable for PCA.

Table 5 presents a correlation matrix of the 18-item Ryff Psychological Well-being Scale. An examination of the inter-item correlations between various pair items showed none exceeding 0.5. Those inter-item correlations indicated that each item of the Ryff Psychologic Well-being Scale measured a different concept.

The Kaiser-Myer-Oklin value was 0.757, exceeding the recommended value of 0.6 (Kaise, 1960, 1970, 1974), and Bartlett's Test of Sphericity (Bartlett, 1950, 1954) reached statistical significance ($p < 0.0001$), supporting the factorability of the correlation matrix (See also Hair et al., 2018; Table 6).

Table 6

KMO and Bartlett's Test

Kaiser-Meyer-Olkin Measure of Sampling Adequacy.		.757
Bartlett's Test of Sphericity	Approx. Chi-Square	1259.325
	df	153
	Sig.	<.001

The Total Variance examination provides a quantitative assessment of the clusters and contribution of each item in the 18-item scale. An Eigenvalue of 1 and beyond indicates that the item making a real contribution to the intended scale. Based on Table 7, six components had an Eigenvalue exceeding 1. The six items explain 56.2% of the variance in the Ryff Psychological Well-being Scale. The Scree plot revealed a clear break after the sixth component, after which the graph flattens (Figure 2), which means the items that fall below this break can be discarded or approached with caution in the analysis.

Table 7

Total Variance Explained for Ryff Psychological Well-being Scale

Component	Initial Eigenvalues			Extraction Sums of Squared Loadings		
	Total	% of Variance	Cumulative %	Total	% of Variance	Cumulative %
1	3.399	18.884	18.884	3.399	18.884	18.884
2	1.793	9.961	28.845	1.793	9.961	28.845
3	1.543	8.572	37.417	1.543	8.572	37.417
4	1.260	7.000	44.417	1.260	7.000	44.417
5	1.086	6.034	50.451	1.086	6.034	50.451
6	1.039	5.772	56.223	1.039	5.772	56.223

7	.904	5.020	61.244
8	.827	4.593	65.837
9	.774	4.299	70.136
10	.746	4.142	74.278
11	.707	3.930	78.209
12	.668	3.709	81.918
13	.639	3.549	85.467
14	.607	3.370	88.837
15	.582	3.234	92.071
16	.540	3.002	95.074
17	.459	2.551	97.625
18	.428	2.375	100.000

Extraction Method: Principal Component Analysis.

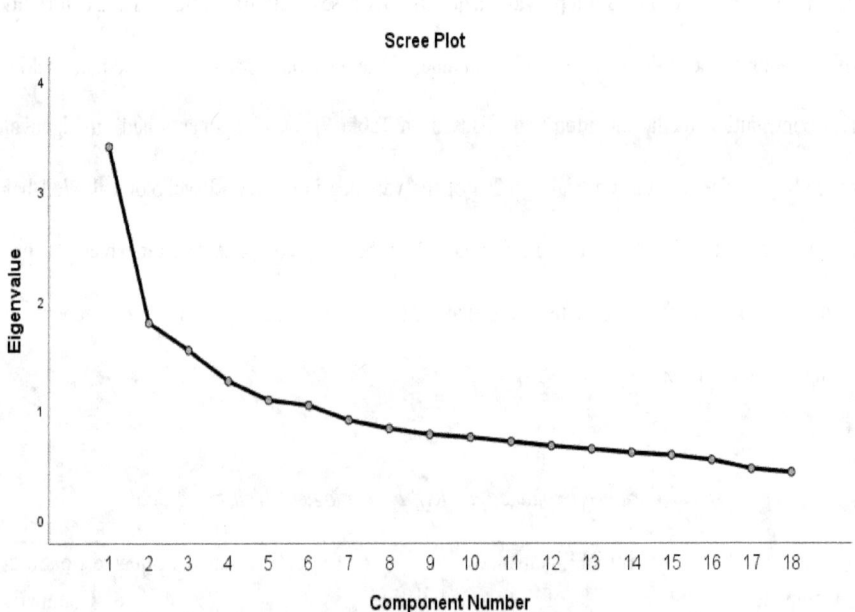

Figure 2. Scree plot of Ryff Psychological Well-being Scale.

Communalities are used to assess the number of variables accounted for in the component captured by each item. Table 8 presented commonalities for the 18-item scale. When the value for the communality is less than 50%, the item can be excluded from the indexation. In that case, six items had a value less than 0.5 or 50%. However, on examination of the six items, only item 15 is less than 0.5 as the others could be rounded up to 0.5. Hence, only item 15 should be excluded from the factor analysis indexation.

Table 8
Communalities for Ryff Psychological Well-being Scale

	Initial	Extraction
Q1	1.000	0.644
Q2	1.000	0.561
Q3	1.000	0.477
Q4	1.000	0.540
Q5	1.000	0.593
Q6	1.000	0.568
Q7	1.000	0.556
Q8	1.000	0.489
Q9	1.000	0.449
Q10	1.000	0.607
Q11	1.000	0.567
Q12	1.000	0.641
Q13	1.000	0.644
Q14	1.000	0.459
Q15	1.000	0.412
Q16	1.000	0.591
Q17	1.000	0.620
Q18	1.000	0.702

Extraction Method: Principal Component Analysis.

Using Promax rotation of factors, the internal reliability of the 18-item was good (> 0.7) and the Total Variance Explained as well as all the other PCA tests supports the suitability and appropriateness of the using the Ryff Psychological Well-being Scale to assess mental health of Jamaican social media users. The Cronbach alpha coefficient was 0.703 which is just above Nunnally's 0.7 threshold, and this according to many scholars is acceptable reliability statistics (Kraiser, 1958, 1960; Horn, 1965; Tabachnick & Fidell, 1998, 2007; Brillinger et al., 2004). However, on disaggregating the overall 18-item scale into six sub-scales found by this study, the Cronbach alphas were low for all (See Table 9). Based on the short form of the Ryff PWBS, the overall scale can be used to suitably and appropriately measure the mental health of Jamaican social media users, and not sub-scales as none of them are at least moderately good for assessment (> 0.6)

Table 9

Internal Reliability Analysis of the sub-scales and overall scale of the Ryff PWBS

Details	Cronbach alpha
Autonomy	0.294
Environmental Master	0.553
Personal Growth	0.416
Positive Relations	0.486
Purpose in Life	0.194
Self-Acceptance	0.544
Overall (PWBS)	**0.703**

The Ryff's Psychological Well-being Scale for this study

Table 10 presents the frequencies for the Ryff's Psychological Well-being S for the sampled respondents. Ryff's PWBS ranges from 0 to 126 (the maximum Likert scale value is 7 and there as 18 questions, which means the total possible outcome is 126). Lower interval scores denote lower psychological well-being or mental health and the versa is equally the case Based on the frequencies, the arithmetic mean is 86.9±9.3, 95%CI: 86.1 - 87.6, with the maximum being 126. Based on the findings, 41.6% (n=224) of the sampled respondents have below-average psychological well-being or mental health status. On the other hand, 58.4% (n=315) of the sampled respondents had at least average psychological well-being or mental health status, with 16.3% (n=88) of the sampled respondents having moderate-to-excellent psychological well-being or mental health status.

Table 10

Ryff's Psychological Well-being Scale or Mental Health Status Scale

Details	n	%
< 61	3	0.56
62 - 64	0	0.00
70 - 74	30	5.57
75 - 79	71	13.17
80 - 84	120	22.26
85 - 89	124	23.01
90 - 94	91	16.88
95 - 99	55	10.20

100 - 104	27	5.01
105 - 109	13	2.41
> 112	5	0.93
		100.0

Multivariate Analysis: Modeling Ryff's Psychological Well-being of Social Media User

The assumptions of multiple linear regression were examined before an ordinary least square regression was modelled with the data. Based on Figures 3 and 4, the assumption of linearity (see also, $F[3, 533] = 5.495$, p-value < 0.001). and normality were met by the data. Two of the critical assumptions of linear regression were upheld, and so this book examines whether social media usage, age, and gender influence Jamaican social media users' psychological well-being or mental health.

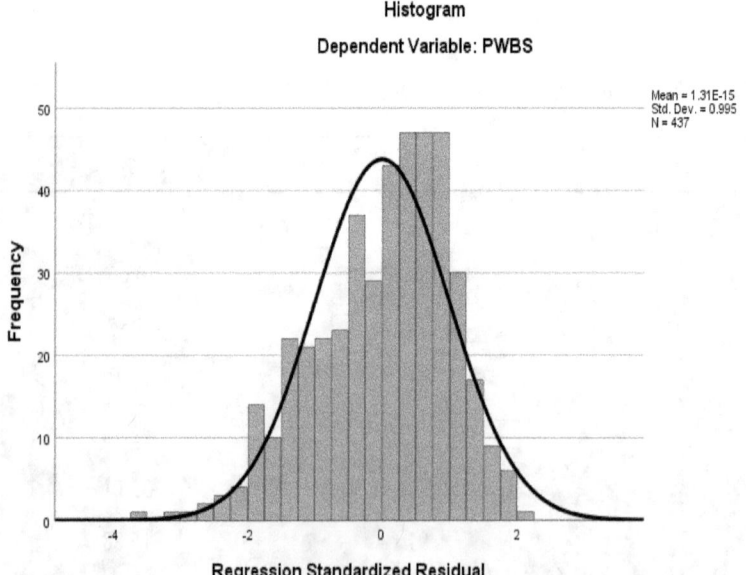

Figure 3: Normality test of Ryff's Psychological Well-being Scale

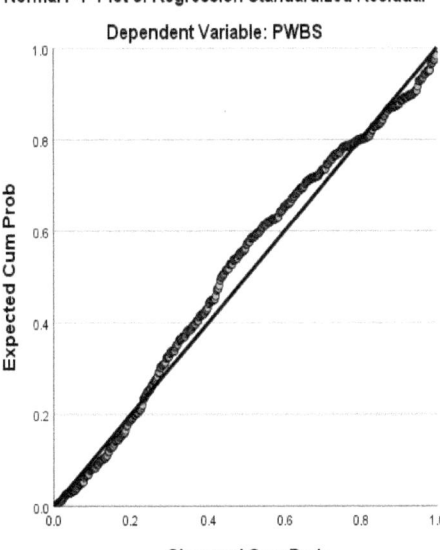

Figure 4: Linearity test for Ryff's Psychological Well-being Scale

With the two critical assumptions of linear regression being upheld, this book test equation [1]:

Ryff's Psychological Well-being = f(Age, Gender, Social Media Usage) ....[1]

Gender was excluded from the model because it had more than 30% of the data points missing. Using multiple linear regression analysis, age and social media usage can linearly be used to model the psychological well-being or mental health status of social media users in Jamaica (F [3, 533] = 5.495, p-value < 0.001), with the linear factor accounting for 3.0% of the changes in psychological well-being or mental health of Jamaican social media users.

Table 11 presents the ordinary least-square (OLS) regression of the psychological well-being or mental health status of Jamaican social media users. The OLS statistical tool showed that age and social media usage (using an average number of hours spent on social media daily). Therefore, the linear model for PWBS is depicted in equation (2):

Ryff's Psychological Well-being = 97.75 - 0.509Social Media Usage + 0.177 Age [2]

An interpretation of equation [2] is there is a positive relationship between age and positive psychological well-being and an inverse association between psychological well-being or mental health and social media usage.

Table 11
Ordinary Least-square (OLS) regression of the Psychological Well-being or Mental Health Status of Jamaican Social Media Users

Model	Unstandardized Coefficients		Beta	t	Sig.	Correlations			Collinearity Statistics	
	B	Std. Error				Zero-order	Partial	Part	Tolerance	VIF
Constant	97.750	3.004		32.542	<.001					
No Of Accounts	-0.060	0.269	-0.011	-0.225	0.822	-0.033	-0.011	-.011	.889	1.124
Age	0.117	0.049	0.118	2.415	0.016	0.147	0.115	.114	.926	1.080
Active Social Media Account	2.331	1.809	0.064	1.289	0.198	0.024	0.062	.061	.897	1.114
Number of hours on social media daily	-0.509	0.168	-0.148	-3.025	0.003	-0.170	-0.144	-.142	.918	1.089

a. Dependent Variable: PWBS

In summary, the more time Jamaicans spend on social media, the more egatively their psychological well-being influences health.

Interpretation and discussion of findings

In 2005, Owen Morgan editor a book entitled 'Health Issues in the Caribbean' and many of the writers, therein, were Caribbean scholars/researchers. Of the thirty (30) articles and an Introduction as well as the Way Forward, only four (4) were written on healthcare delivery in the Caribbean and the Way Forward. The writers of the four articles on healthcare delivery in the Caribbean and the Way Forward did not include social media and mental health (i.e., Mental Health Policy for the Smaller Caribbean Islands, Emerging Challenges for Mental Health in the Caribbean, and Mental Health in the Caribbean: New Paradigms) by way of a single line. Professor Frederick W. Hickling (2005), a Caribbean psychiatrist, who wrote the article captioned 'Mental Health in the Caribbean: New Paradigms' did not envision including social networking as a feature of mental health. Like Prof. Hickling, Sir George Alleyne, former Chancellor of the University of the West Indies, Mona Campus, on examining the health space of the Caribbean, did not see it fitting to include social media and its possible impact on mental health. On examination of the literature on social media usage and/or mental health, no study emerged in the Caribbean on the role that social media usage is having on the populous. This book provides a research-based approach to social media and mental health discourse from a Jamaican perspective.

Discussion

In this book on mental health and social media usage, the Ryff Psychological Well-being Scale (Ryff's PWBS) plays a critical role in answering the research question as to whether social media usage among Jamaicans influences their mental health, and how it does so. The purpose of Ryff's PWBS was to assess the mental health status of people. The developer of Ryff's PWBS (Professor Carol Ryff; Ryff, 1989a, 1989b, 1989c) along with co-developer/s (Ryff & Singer, 2006; Ryff & Keyes, 1995) argued that greater value-outcome for Ryff's PWBS means higher psychological well-being or higher mental health status. There are three versions of Ryff's

PWBS: 1. The Short Version has 18 items, 2. The Medium Version has 19-53 items, and the Long Version has 54 items. Many scholars have examined the psychometric properties of Ryff's PWBS and there were two sides to the discussion, with more studies validating the internal reliability of the scale (Seifert, 2005; Springer & Hauser, 2006; Springer, et al., 2006).

Using a sample of 768 respondents (279 women and 489 men), Garcia et al. (2023) validated the 18-item Swedish version of Ryff's Psychological Wellbeing Scale. They opined, "The results supported the internal consistency and concurrent validity of the 18-item Swedish version. Moreover, invariance testing showed similar measurement precision by the scale across gender. Finally, we found several items, especially the purpose in life item "I live life one day at a time and do not think about the future," that might need revision or modification to improve measurement (Garcia et al., 2023, pp. 1 & 2). Like Garcia et al. (2023), this book concurs with the overall suitability and appropriateness of using Ryff's PWBS to assess psychological or mental health status (Cronbach alpha equals 0.7 or 70% and the analysis in the Principal Component Analysis (PCA)); but that one item could be deleted from the indexation, "I tend to be influenced by people with strong opinions" and it Garcia et al.'s work it was "I live life one day at a time and do not think about the future".

Springer, et al. (2006) questioned the validity of the 6-item subscale of Ryff's PWBS. They postulated that the Short Version of Ryff's PWBS is not sufficient for building those main subscales such as autonomy, environmental mastery, personal growth, positive relations with others, purpose in life, and self-acceptance. In Garcia et al.'s (2023) work, all the subscales were robust enough to adequately assess the previously stated concepts. The multi-dimensional psychometric properties analysis in a book is contrary to the findings in Garcia et al.'s (2023) study. The table, below, presents the findings for the Cronbach alphas for the subscales of this book, and there is evidence that none of the subscales are suitable and appropriate to measuring the subscales. Generally, Ryff's PWBS psychometric properties of 18-item are good to measure overall PWBS or mental health status; but not the subscales. This book concurs with Springer, et al. (2006) findings that the subscales for Ryff's 18-item Version of the PWBS are insufficient items to mean the various intended concepts. This brings into question the validity and internal reliability of the psychometric properties of even the 33-item Ryff's PWBS (i.e. Gao & McLellan, 2018) as they lack enough items in the subscales; but not for the overall multidimensionality of the 33 items. According to Gao and McLellan (2018), "Findings of the present study echoed several previous studies which reported inadequate reliability and validity of Ryff's scales. Given the evidence, it was suggested that future adolescent studies should seek to develop more age-specific and context-appropriate items for a better operationalisation of Ryff's theoretical model of psychological well-being" (p. 1), This book concurs with the general literature that 18 items Ryff's PWBS is generally valid and reliable; which is not the case for the subscales.

Table
Psychometric Properties of the Subscales and Overall Scale of Ryff's PWBS

Details	Cronbach alpha
Autonomy	0.294
Environmental Mastery	0.553
Personal Growth,	0.416
Positive Relations with Others	0.486
Purpose in Life,	0.194
Self-acceptance	0.544
Overall	**0.703**

This book only utilises Ryff's Psychological Well-being Scale (PWBS) to assess mental health, and the subscales were not used because of the low reliability found in psychometric properties. The findings that emerged from this book concur with the literature that social media use influences one's mental health. Zsila & Reyes. (2023) found that social media usage plays a dual role in mental health status. They opined, "The use of social media significantly impacts mental health. It can enhance connection, increase self-esteem, and improve a sense of belonging. But it can also lead to tremendous stress, pressure to compare oneself to others, and increased sadness and isolation. Mindful use is essential to social media consumption" (p. 1).

This book clarifies the relationship between social media usage and mental health status. The current findings revealed that the number of social media accounts does not impact Jamaicans' mental health, but the number of hours spent on social media networks adversely influences the mental health of Jamaicans. Social media usage is creating stressors among Jamaicans as they continue to consume more of this product. The five major social networking sites visited by Jamaicans are Instagram, LinkedIn, WhatsApp, Facebook and Quora, and these are enlarged non-research truth-based educational networks.

CHAPTER 6

CONCLUSION

Social networking has substantially transformed the traditional human communication modus operandi and social interaction (Pantic, 2014), and people are having to deal with a new paradigm. In this new paradigm, people face many challenges and some of them are exposing them to various stressors such as social isolation, inadequacies, dissatisfaction, anxiety, depression, and suicidal thoughts (Dick, 2013; Hamilton, et al., 2015; HelpGate.org, 2023; Kotenko, 2013; Seo, et al., 2021; Thomas, 2012; Williams, 2013). Even though there are positive thoughts about social media usage (HelpGate.org, 2023), the psychological drawbacks cannot be overlooked. The issues of anxiety, depression, and suicidal thought issues are by-products of social media usage (HelpGate.org, 2023; Khalaf et al., 2023), which impairs people's psychological well-being. This book concluded that excessive social media usage influences Jamaicans' psychological well-being or their mental health and not merely using social media.

Psychological -being is a positive mental status and functioning well, which includes happiness and life satisfaction (Diener, 1985, 2000; Diener, et al., 2009; Ruggeri, et al., 2020). Diener et al. (2009) referred to it as positive and negative feelings as well as positive thinking. Social media usage creates positive Social health functioning, and Jamaicans are caught in an era in which their consumption of this social networking space is destroying their mindset and mood.

There is consensus around the general concept of psychological well-being, which is mental health status, such as happiness, positive feelings, and life satisfaction. Psychological well-being is one of the dimensions of health (WHO, 1948a, 1948b), and Tan et al. (2019) indicated that it is a 'core feature' of mental health. Therefore, when this study utilizes Ryff's psychological well-being scale to assess the mental health status of Jamaican social media users, it is suitable and appropriate to do this. The World Health Organization (WHO) conceptualizes mental health as a "state of well-being in which the individual realizes his or her abilities, can cope with the normal stresses of life, work productively and fruitfully, and …[can] contribute to his or her community." This means that psychological well-being scales are suitable and appropriate for assessing mental health status, and in this book, Ryff's 1assessing psychological well-being scale was used to assess the mental health of Jamaica.

Psychological well-being is positive health or good mental health (Ryff, et al., 2004). This conceptualization holds the key to understanding the two types of psychological well-being (Hedonic and Eudaimonic). Hedonic well-being deals with the subjective feelings of happiness. Carruthers & Hood (2004) note that hedonic well-being has two components, an affective and a cognitive component. The affective component deals with positive and negative feelings and the cognitive component looks at satisfaction with life. Eudaimonic well-being refers to the purpose of psychological well-being. Carol Ryff developed and spent years assessing the psychological well-being of different populations (1989a, 1989b, 2014; Ryff & Keyes, 1995). This book provides a research-based finding on the psychological well-being of social media users in Jamaica. The current study found that 41.6% (n=224) of Jamaican social media users' psychological well-being or health status was below average.

The psychological well-being scale developed by Ryff measures the concept of happiness, life satisfaction, and positive affect (Ryff, 1989a, 2014). The original indexation had internal consistencies of 0.86 to 0.93 (Ryff, 1989a). The scale at the time comprised six scales. Ryff's psychological well-being scale has a different number of items. One comprises 18 items (short form) and another 42-84 items (long form). Ryff's Psychological well-being scale has been validated in different nations including China (Cheng & Chan, 2005; Gao & McLellan, 2018; Li, 2014; Kline, 2015), Sweden (Garcia, et al., 2023; Lindfors, et al., 2006), Canada (Clarke, et al., 2001), Iran (Khanjani et al., 2014), Portugal (Fernandes et al., 2010), and Italy (Sirigatti et al., 2009). The current book found that the 18-item Ryff's psychological well-being scale is suitable and appropriate for assessing the psychological well-being of Jamaican social media users; but, the six subscales that comprise three items cannot be used to assess the intended concepts outlined by Ryff.

Although Ryff's psychological well-being scale has been validated in various nations, there are criticisms levied against it, particularly the 18-item version. A group of researchers indicated that the discriminant validity of the 18-item scale is questionable as five of the six items had high cross-loadings (Hsu, et al., 2017). Hambleton and Jones (1993) noted that the true score upon which the Classical Test Theory (CTT) is based showed signs that they do not reflect the responses of the participants. Such a fact decreases the predictability of the specific items. However, Garcia, et al.'s (2023) and Lindfors, et al.'s (2006) works validate the suitability and appropriateness of the 18-item scale. Like studies that questioned the validity of the 18-item Ryff's psychological well-being scale, this book establishes quantitative research-based evidence that the 3 items for explaining the 6 subscales are not adequate in this context. While this book questioned multidimensionality of the Ryff's psychological well-being scale, the overall 18 items are suitable and appropriate in evaluating the general psychological well-being or mental health of social media users in Jamaica.

Bradburn (1969) developed a different measure to assess psychological well-being, which is referred to as the Affect Balance Scale. Bradburn's scale comprises two components. These are one, Positive affective, and two. Negative affect, with each having 5 items. The responses were either yes or no. Bradburn's scale measured happiness. Like Ryff's psychological well-being scale, there were criticisms against Bradburn's scale (McDowell & Praught, 1982). One of the criticisms of Bradburn's psychological scale was it did not adequately summarize the data (Perkinson, et al., 1994). This statistical weakness explains the development of scales. Despite this criticism, Macintosh (1998) argued that is it widely validated and utilized to assess social psychological well-being in many nations (see also, George, 1981; Glatzer & Gulyas, 2014; Harding, 1982; Helmes, et al., 2010; Sauer & Warland, 1982). The many scholars who examined psychological well-being concur that it assesses the mental health status of a human, which is the justification for using Rtff's psychological well-being scale. The researcher is cognizant of other indexes that could have been used, but no foolproof measurement is void of criticism.

The research-based evidence that emerges from this study identifies the impact of excessive social media usage on the mental health of its users. The researcher can make this statement because neither having a social media account did not influence their mental health nor did the number of social media accounts the holder has done not influence psychological well-being or mental health. Shutzmanm & Gershy (2023) referred to excessive social media usage as addiction and that this influences a child's mental health. This explains those who use social media in Jamaica and that is the addiction of the usage that is creating the negative influence on mental health and not the mere usage of social networks.

Zsila & Reyes (2023) opined, "The use of social media significantly impacts mental health. It can enhance connection, increase self-esteem, and improve a sense of belonging. But it can also lead to tremendous stress, pressure to compare oneself to others, and increased sadness and isolation. Mindful use is essential to social media consumption" (p. 1). Social media usage can be likened to alcohol consumption. The drinking of alcohol is not dangerous to one's well-being, it is the excessive consumption of alcohol that is the problem, which is the case for social media usage among Jamaicans.

The excessive usage of social media is a youth phenomenon, and this must be highlighted here. This book found that on average, youth (ages less than or equal to 24 years) daily spent 6 hours± 5 hours on social media. These findings mean that there are youths who spend up to 11 hours daily on social media. The time that youths engage in social networking is affecting their quality of life and the price for this excessive consumption is mental health challenges. This reality in Jamaica concurs with Korean adolescents (Seo, et al., 2021). Seo et al. (2021) postulated, that "...the types of daily life stressors that were positively associated with social media use were sibling rivalry and physical health: (p. 241). The current book is adding mental health to the social media usage discourse as youths are experiencing not only physical health but mental health challenges from their consumption of social networks.

There are three effects of social media usage, a short, medium and a long-term effect. The short-term effect of social media deals with the immediate time. Immediately, social media usage provides new information, knowledge, and social connectivity, improves a sense of belonging, and increases self-esteem (Zsila & Reyes, 2023), which this book refers to as the short-term effect of this phenomenon. In the medium term, social media usage sets a platform for content bullying, negative labelling of others, and a new direction away from knowledge reservoir and repository. McLean Hospital (2023) highlights how social networking has been used for labelling and bullying. This is aptly captured in this sentence, "The social media platform Instagram made headlines last year for suppressing likes to curb the comparisons and hurt feelings associated with attaching popularity to sharing content" (McLean Hospital, 2023). The long-term effect of social media usage is when it begins to create mental health challenges or reduce psychological well-being. McLean Hospital (2023) continued, "But do these efforts combat mental health issues or are they simply applying a band-aid to a wound?" This book shows that the noticeable excessive social media usage of Jamaicans is influencing their mental health because social networking is in a long-term phase for many people.

Karim, et al. (2020) believed that social media is aggravating mental health problems, which assumes that the content bullying, anxiety, and negative labelling of others did not have any effect on people. This book does not support the notion of aggravating mental health challenges, it is forwarding that social networking is creating new psychological challenges in humans. The research-based evidence of this book is that excessive social media usage is negatively impacting the mental health of Jamaicans. This is the rationale why, the book does not support Karim et al.'s perspective that, "Social networking is a crucial element in protecting our mental health." (p. 2) as this contradicts the research-based evidence of this study.

Jamaicans are vulnerable to social media usage, which extends beyond young people. The American Psychological Association (2022) indicated that young people's brains are more vulnerable to social media. The rationale for the perspective of the American Psychological Association is an understandable one and it cannot be discounted because of the benefits of social networking platforms. The American Psychological Association (2022) opined, "Younger social media users are more likely than older ones to have body image issues, while kids who use Instagram or Snapchat before age 11 face a higher risk of online harassment ". Those issues extend beyond young people to everyone, and when these issues happen to people with lower self-esteem, it creates anxiety, depression, social exclusion, and even suicidal thoughts.

In conclusion, it is not merely using social media that negatively influences Jamaicans' mental health status; but it is the excessive usage that creates this challenge. On average, Jamaican youths (less than 25 years old) consume between 5 and 12 hours of social media daily and this offers an insight into excessive usage of social networking platforms. Jamaican adults, on the other hand, consume between 3 and 7 hours of social media daily, and seniors between 2 and 5 hours daily. Jamaican society is at a crossroads as there are no plans afoot to address the social media addiction among young people, and how to deal with the declining mental health because of the excessive usage of the various platforms.

CHAPTER 7
RECOMMENDATION

Social media usage harms Jamaicans, and the youths consume between 5 and 12 hours daily on social networks. Notwithstanding providing information, access to instant interpersonal communication, and access to vast geo-political areas across the globe, excessive social networking usage has become a public health problem in Jamaica. On examination of the literature, Caribbean mental health scholars did not foresee social media to be a future public health challenge and this book provides the research-based context to the new reality. The researcher provides a 5-phase recommendation to address the current findings. These are as followsPhase 1: Sensitization – The findings of this book will be provided to all the major

media houses across Jamaica. Additionally, a copy of the book will be sent to the

Ministry of Health and Wellness as well as the Office of the Prime Minister. A

PowerPoint presentation will be drafted for public consumption, and part of this exercise

will include a discussion on the two main television stations in Jamaica (CVM and TVJ).

The researcher will also extract a 20-page report from the book and this will be for

publication in a reputable online peer-reviewed journal.

Phase 2: Future Research – This book is the premise for future research in the area of

social media usage and mental health. A recommendation for future research is to

examine social networking usage and the mental health of children (i.e., those below

18 years). Additionally, future studies are needed on an appropriate instrument for

measuring the mental health of Jamaicans that can provide suitable sub-scales. This

reality may include a validation of 18-item, 42-item and 54-item Ryff's

Psychological Well-being Scale as well as other scales.

Phase 3: Planning – With the sensitization occurring in society by way of discussions and the provision of the study to policymakers, the researcher will draft a pamphlet on the dangers of social media usage, and collaborate with policymakers to craft an intervention on how to address the harm of social networking on people's well-being. The researcher is an educator who teaches youths, the findings of this study will be presented to the pupils, and they are expected to create a log of their social media usage and how they plan to reduce its effect on their well-being. Furthermore, the researcher will collaborate with a drama group to create a skit on the dangers of social media usage on one's well-being.

Phase 3: Implementation – The researcher will collaborate with the media houses in Jamaica to air the social media danger campaign.

Phase 4: Feedback – The researcher along with his stakeholders will conduct a social media follow-up study to assess the extent of the usage and whether the effect has changed.

www.ingramcontent.com/pod-product-compliance
Lightning Source LLC
LaVergne TN
LVHW020428080526
838202LV00055B/5079